ANITA DESAI

Dimensions of the Inner World

ANITA DESAI

Dimensions of the Inner World

B.L. Tripathi

Prestige

an international publishing house

Published by
Prestige Books
C 3/1, Janakpuri
New Delhi 110 058
Ph. 25507139, 9818755529
Email: prestigebooks@gmail.com
Website: www.asiabookclub.com
ISBN: 81-7551-197-4

Printed at Chaman Offset Press, New Delhi 110 002

Contents

Chapter I

Introduction

Anita Desai (1937) is one of the most prolific writers of serious fiction in Indian English. With *Cry, the Peacock* her literary career began in 1963, although she had been writing and publishing short stories since her adolescence. Her early childhood was spent in Mussoorie and that endowed her with almost a mystic, abundantly romantic sense of connection with the living, teeming world of nature. Her unpretentious childhood would be surrounded by a large number of pets—cats, dogs and birds. Proximity with the natural world crystallizes in her characters overwhelming alertness to flora and fauna, the mystery, beauty and solitude of the nature's bounty. From her cross-cultural upbringing, Indian Bengali father and German mother, she and her siblings inherited wonderful stories, lyrics, music and art that were to form the substance of her writings. Later her study of English literature at Delhi University made her an inveterate and accomplished reader of most of the modern Western literature and inspired her to write in English. She sees English as a language that has been travelling for centuries all over the face of earth and wherever English goes, it seems to adapt itself to those (different) conditions (Signet 1988: 49-50). The spectacular range of her novels: *Cry, the Peacock, Voices in the City* (1965), *Bye-Bye Blackbird* (1971), *Where Shall We Go This Summer* (1975), *Fire on the Mountain* (1977), *Clear Light of Day* (1980), *In Custody* (1984), *Baumgartner's Bombay* (1988), *Journey to Ithaca* (1996), *Fasting, Feasting* (1999), and *The Zigzag Way* (2004) certainly establish her as the pioneer of a new, more radical genre of fiction in India, having conspicuous affinities with international trends and sensibilities.

Undoubtedly her fecund and imaginatively rich portrayals resonate with the finest tradition of the West. Desai's privileged cultural background availed her easy access to the western classics. The novelists who preceded her, R.K. Narayan, Mulk Raj Anand, Raja Rao, and others who were her corollaries also drew their narrative modes as well as notions of the inner world of men and women, from the Western world of knowledge that the literary canons inhabited. Desai's ingenuity lies in lending her observation of life with profound poetic content that makes a sensitive reader feel the touches of Wordsworth, Emily Dickinson, Rimbaud, Rilke, Hopkins, Proust, Virginia Woolf, D.H. Lawrence, and several other proponents of the evolving literary consciousness. In an interview, she puts it, "In my twenties when I first began to work seriously and consciously on my novels, it was D.H. Lawrence, Virginia Woolf, Henry James and Marcel Proust that influenced me more strongly." (Srivastava 1984: 224-25)

Novels and poetry, like other fields of Western knowledge, have been the part of literary culture and aesthetics of the twentieth century societies for their subtlety, imagination and revelations. This truth cannot be debated that the reception of Western mode of knowledge in all fields was not confined to the western readers. Almost all developing, conscious and English educated non-western cultures responded to the modern western literature with alacrity since it exposed with unprecedented impact the innermost labyrinths of the phenomenon, called man in terms that were found identifiable across cultures, ethnicity and nationalities. Thomas Mann's *Magic Mountain* (1924), James Joyce's *Ulysses* (1922) and Virginia Woolf's *To the Lighthouse* (1927) clearly define the history of novel in the twentieth century in their revelations of a more problematic concept of human nature. David Daiches (1970:8) insightfully perceives the difficult struggle of the modern novel with the empirical, existential truths and its endeavour to grasp the fragile, elusive inner core of human psychology:

> Every human being is the prisoner of his own private consciousness, his unique train of association, which results in turn from his own unique past. The public gestures he makes towards communication can never be more than approximate, and he can rely on their being understood. Indeed insofar as the gestures are public, they are bound to be falsified. The signals each individual flashes to the public world are bound to be in some degree misunderstood by the world, because every other person will read them in the light of the person's own history. Society is thus in a sense unreal; its institutions inevitably blunt and coarsen the truth about an individual self, providing means of communication that can distort.

Novel as a European art form became thoroughly global and in India whether in indigenous ethnic languages or in English, the matrices of the novel's narrative were quintessentially drawn from the western models. Western novels shaped our democratic, liberal humanistic sensibility and were naturally recruited as the part of postcolonial culture of the growing Indian educated middle class. The rise of Indian novel in English or novel at large in other languages reveal that the novel began as a European art form, it grew however to become thoroughly global in its conventions drawing its subjects and issues from the indigenous or local contexts.

In the last quarter of the twentieth century and early twenty first, the basic form of novel in the West or India or elsewhere has remained unchanged—untouched by any further experiment. Alan Ryan in "A Growth of a Global Culture" observes that changes there have been, but only in the same direction as the popular culture has taken—greater tolerance of explicit sexual description, a greater acceptance of dysfunctional families, more rapid and violent actions. (Howard & Louis, 1998: 74)

II

In a naturally multilingual India of today, writing or speaking in English is no longer a reflection of alienation from one's roots, or degradation or colonization or incapability for innovation. Since generations, Indians are speaking English. Desai uses it not only as a language of empowerment—having international reach but also as a language of identity of Indian experiences. Her writing in English and the desire to find a new and different territory to question the tradition, going beyond realism, evolving the narrative of consciousness make some critics see her as westernized. In an interview Desai considers erroneous the view that her writing is westernized: "If my writing is westernized there is a whole section of Indian society that is westernized. Whole range of people brought up in urban areas have been exposed to Western ideas through literature." (Uniyal 2000:251) The detailed discussions in the following chapters reveal that she presents Indian cultural practices—even deeply indigenous, local, milieu and landscape with as much competence and familiarity as Nadine Gordimer's rendering of South African subaltern realities. Along with Shashi Deshpande, Nayantara Sahgal and Kamala Markandaya, Desai's engagement with the deeper layers of our cultural institutions, modes of survival of men and women moving through time demonstrate that the novel is the only literary idiom across several languages in India in which women have participated in sufficient number. These writers, however, belonged to a generation that found itself without a systematic history or precedence. It was therefore for them to relate to the history of their culture anew in order to forge in literary terms the consciousness of their gender in the flux of history.

In the late Fifties at a time when chauvinistic values were attached to their sex, writing as woman was still a concept fraught with controversies. Women were confined to low category romantic fiction, published in serialized form in women's magazines in English and other Indian languages, Desai's output immediately drew attention because of its higher standard. Neither callow, mawkish nor sentimental, her stories resonated with humour, poetry, the power of exact image, the ability to be both detached, hard and compassionate, a sense of place, all the strategies of impersonation and finally a historical gaze.

Desai seems to defy most male assumptions of female writing. One of them is that women's style is inferior to that achieved by male novelists, since the female writer cannot transcend the limitation of the immediate: the beginning of a woman's work is generally the writing of a personal diary. Secondly the popular view that the woman's heroine is always a glorified version of herself and therefore she is further restricted by the narrowness of her perception and understanding. Thirdly that a passion for detail is the distinguishing mark of nearly every female novelist. That is, the woman's novels are also deficient in construction, since their authors cannot take the broad view, the female intellect cannot strain so far, it is the neutrality of the artistic mind which the female novelists seem to find it too difficult to realize. In the West, male advice to women writers that they should confine themselves to miniature had been made an issue of controversy. Louise Bernikow (1974: 8) notes, "A woman writer constantly pits herself against cultural expectations of 'womanhood' and women's writing; it becomes necessary for a woman to overcome her sex to write."

In India, however, during the period Desai started writing, it was an established norm that women were inferior writers. She became a conspicuous presence because of her gender and like her other contemporaries was subjected to condescending or generalized opinions. D.S. Maini discerns in Desai moments of lyric beauty and intensity but lacking in great scenes, "no great inventions of events and episodes that bring out the dramatic potential of her characters." Maini proceeds to observe that so long her moral vision remains subservient to the poetic and metaphysical urges of her imagination, there cannot be much hope for her development (1977: 119-20). Being a Henry James scholar Maini seems to evaluate Desai by the parameters of James's novels as "high drama of consciousness."

Desai's spectacular growth since the 1960s when her first novel *Cry, the Peacock* was published is worth watching. True to the genre of women's writing across the globe, Desai's commitment to an individual's perception of a situation turned upside down the valorized notions of "character"; consciousness preceded and prevailed over 'character." Her narrative of consciousness dispenses with plotting action-packed drama in favour of capturing the lived, felt intense moments in the lives of men and women questing for identity. The analysis of novels in the following chapters will reveal that the intimate glimpses into diverse kinds of lives are not without the strain of moral questioning or spiritual struggle for right conduct. Her stories may not outwardly wear their messages, because of the imbedded irony. Truth always exists within the creation of her narrative itself as a contingent uneasy harmony. In the interiority of her characters, Desai discerns unimagined dimensions and relates them with elegiac compassion and tenderness. Although she admits in an interview her intense self-consciousness in translating some ethnic Indian rituals like a wedding ceremony or a funeral, her grasp of typically Indian rituals, cultural practices, social codes, education system, the configurations of class, gender and caste in Indian society testifies to her ability to imaginatively participate in diverse social practices and beliefs. Sarla's disgruntled life of endless fatigue and uninspiring domesticity in a rural dusting town in *In Custody* or Uma's story of corrosive patriarchal oppression and the resultant psychic annihilation in *Fasting, Feasting* could by no means be the narrator's personal account and yet, she seems to identify the characters as if in states of self-introjection; the novel is an illustration of "a woman writer's wider evolution of self-awareness that finds its direction of self-expression relative to a dominant society" (Showalter 1977: 11).

It is perhaps Desai's acute self-consciousness as well as detachment that makes her probe and enter into the culture specific moments or cross-cultural sensibilities with psychological realism. Her narrative therefore brings into being fully realized characters, fully realized social contexts, patterns of behaviour; rich, intricate and alive; description of landscape, both Indian and foreign or even an obscure small town, Deven's Mirpore. Maya's solipsistic introversions and grief of lovelessness, Bim's claustrophobic self-doubts, Nirode's obsessive cynicism, Deven's underdog status, Nur's obscene profligacy and Sita's passionate dedication to her anonymity and autonomy spring from Desai's sense of belonging to India and not just empathy—knowing deeply, intuitively and caring sincerely. Nadine Gordimer's (1975: XXI) perception of herself, her ability to enter into entirely different experiences with amazing familiarity as well as detachment applies to Anita Desai also. Gordimer puts it thus:

> Because the observation, heightened beyond the normal, that implies extraordinary disinvolvement, rather a double process, excessive preoccupation and identification with the lives of others and at the same time monstrous detachment, for identification brings the superficial loyalties (that is to the self) or concealment and privacy, while detachment brings the harsher fidelities (to the truth about the self or revealment and exposure).

Desai does imbibe the posture—both of standing apart and being fully involved that enables her to see in the lives of people a lot more than they can see themselves.

In the novels of intercultural contacts Desai does not appear to be enamoured with the eurocentric cultural ideology or with the point of view of her white characters, nor does she present her Indian characters look pathetic in comparison. Therefore *Journey to Ithaca* is by no means worthy of being clubbed with Gita Mehta's *Karma Kola*.

The most recent novel *The Zig-Zag Way* takes its protagonist to moods and states of mind and hidden inward passages. Into the uncanny quietude, Eric taps parts of himself generally observed by routinised life. Like Laila and Matteo of *Journey to Ithaca*, Eric would desire to be "enthralled by some mysterious spell."

The discussion of *Fasting, Feasting* in Chapter V would reveal that if a family is an institute that stifles lives of women in India, in the United States also in varied ways women are exposed to pain of rejection in familial relations. Parents let children down, children are badly parented. Women in India and the West make substantial emotional investment in relation with men. Women are often socialized to develop their sense of self from the relationship. When women feel that the quality of their relationship is poor, it impacts their well being. Men in contrast derive their sense of self worth from the achievement at their work place.

Acerbic satire at the expense of her characters in diasporic relations has not been Desai's forte, as it requires deeper involvement, covert contempt that Desai's compassionate but detached vision does not sanction. Besides it is worth observing that her vision of history and India is as strongly immersed in the ethos of Indian culture as that of Raja Rao, Kamala Markandaya, R.K. Narayan and Salman Rushdie. All of them have chosen to take different artistic directions and the choices of subject matter. Despite being half-German, her fiction collectively forges the consciousness of the terrible fluidity of things human and non-human. *Journey to Ithaca* culminates this consciousness, dormant in several of her earlier texts.

East-West encounter and the immigrant experiences are treated in *Bye-Bye Blackbird* with sureness and as much credibility as Kamala Markandaya in *Nowhere Man*. Desai may not be as intense in her anger, in her indictment of the pathological racism of the British, but both she and Markandaya reveal with poignant touches the "psyche of the unhoused" states (Nelson 1992: XV). *Baumgartner's Bombay*, the story of a German Jew could be read as a poignant tale of homelessness brought about by the racism prevailing during Hitler's regime, the experience of deracination and displacement.

III

Exposure to diverse cultures as an itinerant; and alertness to histories enable Desai to probe with intuitive insight into Indian cultural milieu, varied strata of Indian society—the upper middle class, the middle-middle class, and the poor and deprived. The complex range of her fictional narrative carves and inscribes many dimensions of our plural Indian realities in interaction with Indian subcontinental history as well as global cultural changes. Her core interest nevertheless remains the lives of women. Unlike Kamala Markandaya's *Nectar in a Sieve* and *Two Virgins*, Shashi Deshpande's *Roots and Shadows* and *That Long Silence, The Dark Holds No Terrors*, Nayantara Sahgal's *This Time of Morning*, who have touched subjects like rape and seduction, the female body, gestation and procreation in terms, which were unprecedented, Desai ponders on the theme of love, betrayal, marriage, bereavement and the problems of compatibility, failure in relationship, the issue of maternity, the stigma of barrenness or not bearing male children. In comparison to Shashi Deshpande particularly, Desai takes several perspectives to maternity and women's relation to the childbirth, rearing and caring. Maternal bonding in Deshpande's treatment flows with deep feelings. Like Saru or Sarita in *The Dark Holds No Terrors*, Desai's Maya would seek enormous satisfaction in having a child. When "she had put the inexperienced greedy, sucking mouth [Renu's] to her nipple" (Deshpande, 1980: 147). But Desai would also dare probe into other variations of experiences as in *Where Shall We Go This Summer?* In this context, her Sita is closer to Margaret Drabble's Jane in *Waterfall*:

> to kiss and care for and feed and amuse a small child merely reinforced my sense of division—I felt split between the anxious intelligent woman and the healthy and efficient mother or perhaps less split than divided. (1969: 110)

Desai's ability to get down to brass tacks comes to terms with what it means to be a woman in India in particular in relation to the domestic and familial space which serves both as a nurturer and destroyer of feminine lives. The growth of feminine lives from infancy through adolescence, youth to old age occupy the interest of Desai's outstanding works. Her drawings of women bring to the fore a salutary challenge to most male Indian writers who have dealt with women; she dares to offer her correctives to the male convention of depicting that and shows that femininity is beyond nomenclature. Even though quite a few of her novels assign pivotal roles to male characters, women are always the sub-text or the subterranean unconscious of the text, inevitably so because it is the woman writer whose perspectives define and probe the identity of male characters. It is worth watching that characters like Gautama, Nirode or even Adit and Dev are susceptible to the 'writerly gaze' of the woman novelist who in shifting perspectives takes ironic view of their superior assumption of themselves. However Desai's involvement with some other male characters as Hugo Baumgartner in diasporic situation and Deven as a product of social underprivileged background, and upbringing that failed to foster in him self-confidence and self-reliance lend them the ironic persona of displaced or variant feminized male. The private consciousness of men, women and children, the drives of nature—love, death, sense of facticity—take on a powerful aura in her depiction. Anxious insecurity, brutal murder, neurotic disability, death, criminal assault and violent ends in her confront the complacent conventional Indian reader with the shocking aspects of social and domestic relationship. From *Cry, the Peacock* through *Fire on the Mountain* to *Fasting, Feasting*, she collectively presents a damning critique of patriarchal family and the generic role of woman as a wife and mother; the suffocating demands placed on woman, most often causing the death of their inner selves.

Desai could be seen as ahead of her contemporaries in renewing and re-energizing the words, syntax and transforming the banalities of everyday reality into the work of art. From her first novel to the last, one may discover the growth of her vision in the diversity of her contexts and subject matter. Desai's writings travel across and beyond her given environment, her mores, enter into those territories of experiences that open up infinite secret zones of reality and imagination.

Works Cited

Bernikow, Louise. 1974. "Introduction." *The World Split Open: Four Centuries of Women Poets in England and America*. New York: Harcourt Brace.

Daiches, David. 1970. *The Novel and the Modern World*. Chicago: University of Chicago Press.

Deshpande, Shashi. 1980. *The Dark Holds No Terrors*. New Delhi: Penguin.

Drabble, Margaret. 1969. *Waterfall*. Harmondsworth: Penguin.

Gordimer, Nadine. 1975. *Selected Works*. Jonathan Cape.

Howard Michael and W.M. Louis Roger. 1998 *The Oxford History of the Twentieth Century*. New York: O.U.P.

Maini, Darshan Singh. 1977. "The Achievement of Anita Desai," in *Indo-English Literature: A Collection of Critical Essays*, K.K. Sharma, ed., Ghaziabad: Vimal.

Nelson, S. Emmanuel. 1992. *Rewording: The Literature of the Indian Diaspora*. New York: Greenwood Press.

Robinson, Andrew. 1988. "Interview: Anita Desai," *Saturday Statesman,* 13 August: 2.

Segnet, Pascale. 1988. "An Interview with Anita Desai," *Commonwealth Essays and Studies*, 10, 2.

Showalter, Elaine. 1977. *A Literature of Their Own*. Princeton: Princeton University Press.

Srivastava, Ramesh K. Ed. 1984. *Perspectives on Anita Desai*. Ghaziabad: Vimal.

Uniyal, Ranu. 2000. *The Fiction of Margaret Drabble and Anita Desai: Women and Landscape*. New Delhi: Creative Books.

Chapter II

The Novels of the 1960s: Images of Unaided Isolation

With the publication of *Cry, the Peacock*, Anita Desai received critical acclaim as a writer who initiated psychoanalytical approach to novel writing. Desai's portrayal of Maya in *Cry, the Peacock* and thereafter Nirode, Monisha and Amla in *Voices in the City* infuses the narrative of the novel with images of trauma that unlock the shocking, repressed secrets of mind and reveal the lives lived with unbearable strain and ruined for want of love and understanding. The pages of the two novels invoke the stories of isolation, fearful fantasies, unhinged, traumatized mental states and what comes to the fore with stunning impact is the unaided, misunderstood loneliness of male and female lives.

II

The new grounds Desai breaks in her depiction resonate with psychological realism. The musings of high-strung Maya redolent with symbols of dreams and desire make us behold her past, the early childhood, adolescence and her present. The lyrical prose steers the readers to coordinate the various patterns in the novel and one may see through the vulnerable story-telling self of Maya in consonance with her self-dramatizing persona. Desai's protagonist, Maya, in terms of Indian philosophical system (Singh 1988: 158-59) means the creation of the world which is ultimately unreal. *Maya* is also denoted by the term *Prakriti* which constitutes the seed of the entire phenomenal world and which cannot be defined as real or unreal. "The very nature of *Maya* therefore is contradictory. As *Prakriti*, her fulfilment is in rooting, possessing, sprouting, creating as *Maya* however this phenomenon liberates and is liberating, volatile—free floating. Maya of *Cry, the Peacock* however unlike her true nature can neither fulfil herself as *Prakriti* or liberate herself as *Maya* in a stifling relationship with Gautama. Desai's description of the unharnessed overwhelming longings and growing derangement of Maya turns out to be an innovative contribution to Indian literature at large. The novel drives home the elusive, obscure reasons of discord in man-woman relationship. The title draws us to the analogue between a peacock's cry in the wilderness seeking a companion with Maya's desperate agonized cries for making real genuine human contact, that remains thwarted. Usha Bande's view (1988: 59) that "There is no attempt on her part at self-analysis, to apprehend her demands" is not a correct assessment of Maya, nor are the varied observations of her "father fixation" or "frustrated libidinal instincts." On the other hand Desai gives Maya a distinct individuality, an intuitive moral awareness, sense of justice and a poetic imagination.

Married to Gautama in an oppressive relationship that continues to pester her with the complex of her inadequacy, her childishness inevitably puts strain on the fragile sensitive mind of Maya making her unsure of her sexual and personal identity. Penelope Mortimer's epigraph of her novel *Pumpkin Eater* (1962) describes Maya's situation: "Peter Peter pumpkineater / Had a wife he could not keep her/ He put her in a pumpkin shell / And there he kept her very well." Gautama, described as down to earth, stolid, rational lawyer however is dedicated to the public life and social concerns. The novel begins with the death of Toto, Maya's pet dog. Toto could be seen as a surrogate child to Maya. The narrative puts it: "Childless women do develop fanatic attachment to their pets, they say. It is no less a relationship than that of a woman and her child; no less worthy of reverence, and agonized remembrance" (Anita Desai 1963: 9). Gautama fails to understand this attachment and promises to bring another dog for her. Gautama's advocate associate calls on him and he "rose immediately ordering tea to be sent to the study forgetting her, forgetting her woes altogether" (7). Toto's death may be trivial for Gautama, possessed with a superior assumption of his busy professional life, but it matters to Maya's distraught state of mind:

> Showing how little he knew of my misery, or of how to comfort me. *But then, he knew nothing that concerned me*, . . . telling me to go to sleep while he worked at his papers, he did not give another thought to me. . . . It is his hardness—no, no, not hardness but the distance he coldly keeps from me. His coldness, his coldness, and incessant talk of cups of tea and philosophy in order not to hear me talk and, talking, reveal myself. It is that—my loneliness in this house. (9, my italics)

A motherless child, Maya had been the centre of her father's affection, dependent on her father for the fulfilment of her emotional needs—for love, understanding, compassion. In her adult relationship with Gautama, the gulf between the no-nonsense world of Gautama and Maya's urgencies for emotional attachment becomes visible. Maya laments in the opening pages: "A husband who did not give another thought to me, to either the soft willing body or lonely wanting mind that waited near his bed." (9) Maya's longings are seen as reflective of immaturity and inability to cope with the realities of life. Gautama holds her father responsible:

> —for making you believe that all that is important in the world is to possess, possess—riches, comforts, posies, dollies, loyal retainers—all the luxuries of the fairy tales you were brought up on. *Life is a fairy tale to you still.* What have you learnt of the realities? The realities of common human existence, not love and romance, but living and dying and working, all that constitutes life for the ordinary man. You won't find it in your picture books. And that was all you were ever shown—picture books. . . . And here you are, capable of seeing nothing but delusions, imagining them to be real. How prettily you stroll in your garden dreaming of the fairies that sleep in the buds. (115, my italics)

Gautama used to quoting the *Gita* profusely may be considered right from coolly rational chauvinistic point of view. His wit and wisdom discerns in Maya 'father fixation,' "this is the reason 'why you married me, a man so much older than yourself.'"

(146) The narrative does not reveal whether Maya's marriage was an arranged one or she was married according to her own choice. Gautama's observation could be seen as the usual complacent and self-aggrandizing view men take of themselves. In fact his observations however precise and witty they may sound, are intended to belittle and undermine Maya. As the novel gathers momentum, we infer it is Gautama who is genuinely against Maya's freedom. This apparently utterly conventional good and successful husband is known for his detachment and superiority, for his smug self-importance. Maya's fine sensitivity, tenderness of heart, her terrain of desires, love for nature remains grossly misunderstood. She muses:

> Grey, grey, all was grey for Gautama, who lived so narrowly, so shallowly. And I felt sorry, infinitely sorry for him, for this slow, harmless, guileless being who walked the fresh grass and did not know he touched it. (196-97)

Hallucinations and delusions, sinister images flood her mind: lizards, snakes, the rats sucking their young, albinos. Fear of the unknown threatens her:

> Perish one must. The desert is waiting, the rats and the lizards. They'll claim the flesh, the winds will carry the bones away. Mind the wind. Shut the windows. Hide, hide. (128)

III

The story moves around a prophecy made during Maya's childhood that in the fourth year of her marriage, either she or her husband would die. This episode has received ample attention of the critics. K.R.S. Iyengar while discussing the novel notices the ominous fatality in these words: "Over the whole narrative in *Cry, the Peacock*, which is really Maya's effort to tell her story to herself, to discover some meaning in her life, and even to justify herself to herself, over the whole narrative there hovers an uncannily oppressive sense of fatality." (1973: 465)

Belief in fatalism, motivated by astrological predictions or by the fact that human life is subjected to mysterious, unresolved contingencies has been accepted a universal archetypal phenomenon. Maya's traditional Brahmin family believes in astrological matching before settling marriage:

> Born of a family of Brahmins that for generations . . . according to the prescribed patterns, had married according to the advice and suitability of their horoscopes, had diligently taken up careers that the pundits had chosen for them out of the constellations, had had their children's stars studied and speculated upon. (75)

The prophecy plays an important role in the married life of Maya who broods over it and is never able to forget it completely. As a small child her Ayah took Maya to an albino priest to cast her horoscope and he prophesied:

> My child, I would not speak of it if I saw it on your face alone. But look, look at the horoscope. Stars do not lie. And so it is best to warn you, prepare you. . . . Death . . . to one of you. When you are married—and you shall be married young. . . . Death—an early one—by unnatural causes . . . the child must be persuaded, she must listen to my warning. It is my duty to prepare her, my duty. . .
>
> Four years after your marriage, so the stars prophesy, and the space between your eyes, the mark there, supports this prophecy. I have warned you, performed my duty. Be wary, child, be wary and fear God. (29-31)

The child Maya carries the sharp memory of this sinister prophecy to her adulthood. Gothicized atmosphere of gloom and mystery envelope Maya's life signalling the disturbing return of the past upon present. Memory tortures her. After four years of her marriage she becomes obsessed with the prophecy: "and four years it was now, we had been married four years. . . . I knew the time had come. It was now to be either Gautama or I" (32-33). The stream of consciousness clubbing the past with the present makes this scene figure in section 1 of Pt. II whereas Maya's act of pushing Gautama from rooftop, takes place at the end of Pt. II of the novel. Gautama's violent death has drawn varied critical perceptions. Jasbir Jain takes the view that "Maya pushes Gautama off the roof in order to protect her world of sensuous abundance." (1987: 22) Perhaps living unintruded in her secret world of make-believe makes her sense Gautama as an aloof and hostile enemy, therefore he must die, before he makes her die.

The more realistic observation makes us see through several factors: shortly after the pet dog Toto's death she receives a letter from her brother Arjun from America in which he makes a mention of the prophetic words of the priest, that Maya's mind has inexorably lodged. The shocking act of killing her husband could be seen as motivated by a hopelessness that the Maya-Gautama relationship spells—bearing the strain of his cold treatment during four years of marital life, the inconsolable emotional starvation, she suffers in her craving for love, for intimate contact. The growing desolation of her spirits is revealed in the frustration she keeps experiencing:

> longing to be with him, be close to him . . . make haste in undressing. . . . But when I went . . . he had closed his eyes not with mere tiredness, but in profound, invulnerable sleep, and was very far from any world of mine, however enticing. (93)

Besides marital incompatibility, another factor responsible for aggravating Maya's miseries is the attitude of her mother-in-law. A social worker, the mother-in-law is driven by popular social values. Maintaining appearance—visible public profile is her top priority. She does not permit Maya's dormant maternal potential any outlet. Maya seeks her time, her company to soothe her, but she is never available. The mother-in-law seems to have set the "order" of the family by treating with disdain the basic emotions of love, attachment, compassion, empathy and concern. Mother's "conditioning" has reduced the family incapable of simple joys of life; everything is cerebral and impersonal. In her portrayal one may sense the distortion of femininity by the patriarchal norms. The social-political world to which she belongs has made her internalize values considered significant in male-dominated culture. Political issues, national events preoccupied her milieu. Even to relax, a game of cards would be resorted to. Desai seems acutely aware of the polarized world of chauvinistic male culture separate from the world of women:

> In Gautama's family one did not speak of love, far less of affection. One spoke—they spoke—of discussions in parliament, of cases of bribery and corruption revealed in government, of newspaper editors accused of libel, and the trials that followed, of trade pacts made with countries across the seas, of political treaties with those across the mountains, of distant revolutions, of rice scarcity and grain harvests . . . they had innumerable subjects to speak on, and they spoke incessantly. Sometimes, in order to relax, they played games of cards, so swiftly, so nervously, so intently, that they found they had to release the mounting pressure by conversing, and would begin to talk again, of political scandal and intellectual dissent. (46-47)

The mother-in-law is drawn as possessed with immense energy, harnessed in social work, "like some busy rhinoceros charging through the forest, to her dispensary or her crèche, or her workshop for the blind, the disabled, the unemployed." (47) She is energy incarnate but ironically it is not directed to the crying needs of Maya. Her austere life-style is demonstrated by her meagre meals and dull-coloured clothes, commenting on which Maya says: "In that dark room, I was the only one who wore a sari of bright colour. The rest wore colours that no one could care about." (49) She may be matronly but is incapable of giving motherly love to Maya. She could command respect but not love:

> broad body that was so powerful with the richness and redness of the blood that flowed so abundantly in her. If she was a figure of old age, she was as much a figure of fire and energy. The gods might one day erect a monument to her, though human beings would not. She awed me, and attracted me at the same time. Were she to lift her hands into the sky, from those gnarled tips her blood would flow in generous streams towards those who needed it. I wondered if I was one of them. (158)

The final moments of the narrative disclose subtly how a dominant mother's influence could mould the personality of the children. Any display of overt sentimentality submitting oneself to candid emotional ties was deemed symptomatic of inferior breeding. The family dreaded passion, "as wisemen dread their flesh." (217) The mother could not even form a close bonding with her daughter, Nila. Both living in their private worlds dread lest their private thoughts spill over into the open. They even avoid physical contact, their body language reveals distance.

> They sat there, knee to knee, but scrupulously avoiding contact, in the semi-dark beyond the ring of lamp-light, two black figures in bowed postures, jointed by a thread of white that each held in her hands and worked at, silently, absorbedly. Neither spoke, they dreaded speech now that they were so close together, as though their thoughts and ideas, safe and controlled by each one within herself, would explode out of the bounds prescribed for them and spill into the open, were the two to meet and touch. They dreaded this as their son and brother had dreaded passion, as wise men dread their flesh. (216-17)

It is easy to discern that the women like Maya's mother-in-law are merely agents of the male-dominated social processes. Maya's sister-in-law (husband's sister) and her mother-in-law visit her for a short period which proves invigorating for Maya simply because she does not have such company and for that short period she forgets her marital woes and her personal miseries. But the mother-in-law is too preoccupied with her busy schedule. She is more concerned with social welfare than with the welfare of her own daughter-in-law and, by implication, of her son. Maya entreats her to stay for a few days more. She earnestly needs her company: "If they stayed a while, they might help me, as my own father could not by teaching me some of that marvellous indifference to everything that was not vital, immediate and present. I did not know how they could do this, but somehow it had to be done." (162) Maya being motherless craves for maternal tenderness and emotional refuge in her mother-in-law: "and yet I yearned for her to hold me to her bosom. I could not remember my own mother at all." (163) When Maya implores her to stay, she says "How can I, child?" she said, smiling and then frowning, "It is impossible." (163) It is ironic that her own daughter's marriage is on the rocks and she is contemplating divorce for which she needs Gautama's professional help but he callously refuses to be of any help.

> What does she take me for, one of those two-rupee lawyers that squat under the banyan tree outside the courts. . . . I haven't time to waste on a case like hers—the mess she makes by being too bossy and self-willed and bullying. (161-62)

IV

The novel touches several issues and most importantly childlessness, considered a social stigma. The portrayal of Maya is also a vehicle of critiquing the dogmatic norms of patriarchy. For infertility, it is always the woman who is blamed and not the man. Besides, the woman's inability to produce a son is also assumed to be a social stigma. The androcentric culture breeds in women the desire to beget male child. Pom goes to the temple with offering to the deity in the hope of getting a son. Mrs. Lal who has four daughters is pregnant again in the hope of getting a son. Reacting to Mrs. Lal's condition, Maya vehemently feels:

> I ought to have been able to rejoice at this, as my father had rejoiced in me, saying that in a daughter, he had treasure. Yet now the word brought up visions of dowries, of debts, humiliations to be suffered, and burdens so gross, so painful that the whole family suffered from them. (71)

Maya's story encloses several other tales. Arjun, Maya's brother, has been a rebel since the very beginning and refuses to be taken as the son of Rai Sahib. He behaves against the expectations of his father and ultimately runs away to the U.S. to try his luck all on his own, as an unknown citizen, and the other is a teacher friend of Maya, Leila who teaches Persian in a Girls' College on a meagre salary nursing her petulant, temperamental, irritable, terminal tubercular husband. The early part of the novel invokes a subtle comparison of Maya and Arjun in the bird imagery: "If I was a partridge, plump, content, he was a wild bird, a young hawk that could not be tamed, that fought for its liberty." (134) Arjun obviously seeks his freedom being in a privileged position because of his gender: potentially too strong to be fettered by easy life and prosperous background, a person who would like to stand on his own. The comparison is also suggestive of the marked difference in the upbringing of Maya and Arjun. The greater tenderness with which Maya was brought up made her dependent on others while the brother was made to depend on his own resources. The novel diagnoses the way in which concept of 'femininity' makes women subject to the power of the father and then of husband.

Another extremity of feminine oppression is manifest in Leila who, against the wishes of her parents, elopes with her lover who is a tubercular. She suffers his taunts and tantrums simply because he is her husband, however worthless he may be. She is a masochist, one who derived pleasure from her own pain and humiliation and "was one of those who require a cross, cannot walk without one." (58) She is the real fatalist and she accepts it. She simply accepts her lot pointing her fingers towards the centre of her forehead, "It is all written in my fate long ago." (59) Leila is one who resigns herself to fate without any remonstrance. Maya does not appreciate this downright surrender "had she raged, revolted, I should have rushed to her now." (59)

Maya's perspectives present a range of characters to the readers and we perceive in Maya a sensitive human core. She is certainly not a passive, obsessed, arrested in childhood, child woman, she possesses a mind of her own, the potential to be a loving, caring independent woman. She like Laila, as she admits, would not surrender to her fate, but the relentless, continued aloofness of her husband and her confinement, straitjacketing has stripped her of a sense of self-worth and that brings about her deterioration and a recognition that life fails to offer her any solace:

> God now I was caught in the net of the inescapable, and where lay the possibility of mercy, of release? . . . Am I gone insane? Father! Brother! Husband! Who is my saviour? I am in need of one. I am dying and I am in love with living. I am in love, and I am dying. God let me sleep, forget, rest. But no, I'll never sleep again. There is no rest anymore—only death and waiting. (97-98)

The volatile imaginings flash in Maya's hysterical mind an idea:

> The man [Gautama] had no contact with the world, or me. What would it matter to him if he died and lost even the possibility of contact. What would it matter to him. (175)

Pushing Gautama from the rooftop is unleashing the volcanic content of her repressed psyche. But the act also destroys her. She suffers mental breakdown and regresses in the world of childhood at her father's home.

V

Voices in the City juxtaposes the city of Calcutta with the chart of Nirode's life. The novel, as the blurb suggests, invokes the din, the clamour, the mercenary indifferent nature of the city, its corrosive effects upon a family. Brought up in luxury by an over-indulgent mother, Nirode settles down in Calcutta and adopts a Bohemian life, while his elder sister, Monisha, leads a servile existence within the rigid confines of a traditional Hindu family. Their younger sister arrives from Bombay and becomes involved with an artist, but the outcome of this and the dreadful decision Monisha eventually takes, make this novel a doubly haunting and consummate work of art. Divided into four sections: 'Nirode,' 'Monisha,' 'Amla' and 'Mother,' the novel explores the lives of the artists: the failed artist Nirode, the would-have been artist Monisha, the would-be artist Amla and the artist established Dharma who has been able to strike a balance between art and life. The novel nevertheless focuses on Nirode. The brother and two sisters are the product of a seemingly disintegrated family that their mother failed to hold together. In their narrative movement between the past and the present, we discover their individual history. As adults in the city of Calcutta, they find themselves caught in the cross-currents of urban culture and its contradictions. The novel also draws in kaleidoscopic images the cultural transition of India in the 1950s—a phase in which the older elements are not altogether dead, and the emergent ones not fully evolved. The narrative describes the life of a feudal family of Kalimpong dominated by the mother, an inferior father who is most of the time drunk and four children, two sons and two daughters—Arun, Nirode, Monisha and

Amla. With Arun's departure to England for higher studies begins the novel. We get to know of Nirode who works in a newspaper office as a clerk, not holding an important position. Monisha is married to Jiban, a middle-rung officer in a Government Department with a large joint family, a typical middle class family. The younger sister Amla has received training as a commercial artist in Bombay and has come to Calcutta to join an advertisement firm. The death of the father renders mother lonely when all the children are outside Kalimpong: she seeks the amicable company of her neighbour, one retired Major Chaddha with whom, as her children assume, she was also having an affair. This relationship stirs deep resentment in Nirode. Nirode's hostility to his mother is manifest in not only refusing to read her letter but also employing filthy vituperatives against her, suspecting her of having several illicit relations. His anger never remains contained: "Raising himself on an elbow which shakes and trembles with the pressure of his shrunken body, he speaks with ferocity. Tell her to go to show up that old Major of hers, all share of banks or finance or insurance, and all the rest of her bleeding equipment." (Anita Desai 1965:73)

Nirode's life has been a succession of failures in whatever he tried, from bringing out a magazine called *Voice* to writing of a play, opening a book stall, and even selling spurious antique art pieces. He has had a close brush with death when he was critically ill but was hospitalised and nursed by Monisha. Amla has an infatuation with a married artist Dharma and through her we are shown the world of the upper class society. Monisha's ill-matched marriage, her loneliness, sterility, the stress of living in a joint family and an unresponsive husband push her to the breaking point and she commits suicide by self-immolation. The novel ends with the funeral of Monisha after the arrival of the mother from Kalimpong.

Desai's narrative employs the metaphors of European naturalism to project the seamy side of the under-privileged sections and to debunk the wide hiatus that exists between one class and the other, the hypocritical norms of class-consciousness. One may read in the plight of Nirode, Amla and Monisha the anxious quest of the artists for some meaning amidst the panorama of futility. Seema Jena puts it: "Since no metalled high-way exists for the artist's journey, the writer has shown different wandering ways and tortuous lanes, the artists of various shades and temperaments take and the relation they have with the society." (1989: 45) The urban metropolitan consciousness comes into being in the voices of the three representatives of great Indian middle class. The urban circumstances and compulsions lock the characters in a closed world without promising release or a viable alternative. J.P. Tripathi's view attributes the depression of Nirode, Monisha's helplessness or Amla's predicament to the city of Calcutta: "a kill joy city . . . has an intrinsically negative anarchistic genius demonstrating '*Cholbe na*' till the point of annihilation." (1986: 26-27). The urban life manifests itself through the newspaper and the institution of family. Newspaper is the most powerful component of establishment, not that it cannot be anti-establishment but in the context of the novel, it is pro-establishment. Before the emergence of electronic mass-media and even after that, the newspaper still remains the most powerful medium of moulding public opinion, hence a lot of industrial houses were taking over newspapers way back in the early 60s. Desai comments on this through Nirode: "There are other more dangerous worlds: lies, hypocrisies, retract, communal, religion. . . . Editors are born without eyes, without pupils or corneas or irises." (30) In spite of his intellectual pretensions, and superciliousness, Nirode's dedication to his individual freedom is basically flawed because it has blocked all roads to genuine illumination; rendered him incapable of any human relationship. Whatever ideology he is holding on to, it has sapped and sopped his human core. Monisha, the quiet, fragile, sensitive, well-read woman knows it and she acknowledges it: "if I had religious faith, I could easily enough renounce all this. But I have no faith, no alternative to my confused despair, there is nothing I can give myself to, and so I must stay." (122)

Nirode's choice of non-conformism, the bohemian life style seems to have been imbibed from his attachment to the existential writers. He quotes Camus, and considers himself an outsider, "an outlawed hermit crab." (190) The irony is that while in the western existential hero one finds a justification of *angst*, there is no valid justification for Nirode's cynicism and negative mind-set. He is charged with negative, destructive energy that precipitates the tragic termination of Monisha. Had he desired, he could have saved her. The narrative astutely describes:

> He had failed, obviously—but where was the will to get up, select another ladder, and begin the journey of absurdity all over again? . . . He had never believed in the magazine so much as to be depressed by its sorry condition. . . . He was wearied by his own unsureness in which he swept back and forth like a long weed undulating under water, a weed that could live only in aqueous gloom, would never rise and sprout into clear daylight. He was proud to the point of being a fanatic, he was intense enough to be capable of whole-hearted dedication—yet he drifted, a shadowy cipher and his life consisted of one rejection following another. . . . There was only this endless waiting, hollowed out by an intrinsic knowledge that there was nothing to wait for. (63-64)

Nirode's objectiveless, unjustifiable anger eats his entrails, like an alcoholic who absorbs lots of unnourishing, false calories which ultimately eat away his intestine and liver. Nirode's visit to Jit and his wife makes him recoil with disgust for marriage:

> Marriage, bodies, touch and torture . . . he shuddered and, walking swiftly was almost afraid of the dark of Calcutta, its warmth that clung to one. . . . All that was Jit's and Sarla's, he decided, and indeed all that had to do with marriage, was destructive, negative, decadent. He could waste no time on it. . . . But strode on, not wasting time. (35)

This loathing for marriage has its origin in the family life of the Rays that remains suppressed. Monisha interprets Nirode's and her own problematic contradictions. Afraid of involvement, both torment themselves in their aloneness:

> I discover in this unattached, drifting bird-creature that vital element that is missing from Nirode and myself—the element of love. And I discover that it is the absence of it that makes us, brother and sister, such abject rebels, such craven tragedians. In place of this love that suffuses the white face of this mystic waif, we possess a

> darker, fiercer element—fear. I see now that both Nirode and I shy from love, fear it as attachment, for 'from attachment arises longing.' (135)

Unlike Nirode, Monisha's introspection lends her a deeper insight into her conditions. Her self-pity however disables her from taking a positive step to overcome her problems.

Nirode refuses to compromise with his individual choice even in the face of hardships. The reason for his leaving the petty clerkship in a newspaper is this that he did not want to do the insignificant job he was assigned. Men like him cannot be reduced to a mere cog in the huge machinery called community. If the novelist would not let the individuality of Nirode be corroded by collectivity, it is not to project him as an ideal hero, but to make us see through his muddled up, false sense of ego that prompts him to denounce every prospect of mitigating his abject condition. Amla's suggestion to ask mother for money who has pots of it, brings about bitter outburst:

> When do little girls get over their mother complexes? That's the worst of having a family—she just one of 'em, even the nicest, and in no time she's signalling to the rest of the clan to come and catch him, catch him and brand him with the family name, family money, family honour. I've given up using a family name, Amla, and I want no more of family life. . . . I'll tell you my ambition, Amla—or, rather, what all my ambitions have come down to: to earn only as much as I need immediately, never so much as to spill into a bank. (156-57)

The extremity of his cynicism is unleashed: "for meals—I scrounge off friends. It's amazing how many willing victims we parasites find ourselves. Society must have some kind of guilt complex about us after all. As for clothes, I haven't needed any for a long time now." (59) In the very beginning of the novel, Nirode clearly says to Bose that he is very different from most of the people:

> You know, Bose, . . . I've reached a point now—I always knew I would arrive at it one day—when it would be impossible, physically impossible to work under any man, by his orders at a given

> time, at a meaningless job. I loathe those automatons at the top—I loathe their superciliousness, their arrogance, their *blindness*. How dare they be arrogant when working at such senseless jobs? Spend their lives, their entire energy and intelligence on some thing that does not matter? How can one? . . . Better to leap out of the window and end it all instead of smearing this endless sticky glue of senselessness over the world. Better not to live. (18)

Nirode's rebellion, disenchantment, deliberate courting of miseries hardly lends any authentic courage and heroism to his persona, his masochism however vitiates the lives involved with him. The narrative resonates with contempt for him, in investing with him the imagery of a long weed, "he swept back and forth like a long weed undulating under water, a weed that could live only in aqueous gloom, would never rise and sprout into clear day light." (63-64)

VI

Monisha with all her sensitivity and intuitive intelligence figures as a fragile character who never fights for her survival, could never make free choices. An introvert, she is capable of making genuine contact with her inner self and yet she withdraws herself into her own shell, secretly suffocates in the bustling and crowded, typical middle class joint family. The snail imagery describes the viscusness of her condition. Her diary discloses a situation fraught with difficulties:

> I'm glad to be occupied in cutting vegetables, serving food, brushing small children's hair. Only I wish I were given some tasks I could do alone, in privacy, away from the aunts and uncles, the cousins and nieces and nephews. Alone, I could work better, and I should feel more—whole. But less and less there is privacy. Even my own room, which they regarded at first as still bridal, now no longer is so (the tubes are blocked, it is no good), and sisters-in-law lie across four-poster, discussing my ovaries and theirs. Kalyani *Di* throws open my wardrobe in order to inspect my *Saris* . . . and sees—my books. The whole wardrobe full of books. To my perplexity, she laughs. . . . I see that . . . there is nothing to laugh at in Kafka or Hopkins or Dostoyevsky or my Russian or French or

> Sanskrit dictionaries. But I wish that they would leave me alone, sometimes, to read. (115-16)

This section of the novel not only portrays Monisha's shattered life as the typical daughter-in-law of the middle class Bengali family but also includes all middle-class and lower middle class married women invoking images of women behind the bars, who with least resistance surrender their individuality and identity to the roles cut out for them. Howsoever enlightened or well-read the daughter-in-law may be, as Monisha is, she has to mould herself into the persona of a respectable daughter-in-law meeting the expectations of the society. Monisha consequently looks at society with "disbelief" (162) Virginia Woolf unleashes her anger at the stereotypes our culture promotes in the interest of patriarchy. That makes inevitable the co-existence of double selves in a woman—one angelic—conforming to the patriarchal values, the other secretly seething with rage, resentment and frustration (Gorden 1984: 9). The image of the woman behind bars is a recurrent image that women writers from Bronte Sisters, Charlotte Perkin Gilman, Edith Wharton to Virginia Woolf employ to reveal the oppression of women. Desai's narrative reveals this:

> I think of generations of Bengali women hidden behind the barred windows of half-dark rooms, spending centuries in washing clothes, kneading dough and murmuring aloud verses from the *Bhagvad-Gita* and the *Ramayana*, in the dim light of sooty lamps. Lives spent in waiting for nothing, waiting on men self-centred and indifferent and hungry and demanding and critical, waiting for death and dying misunderstood, always behind bars, those terrifying black bars that shut us in, in the old houses in the old city. The eyes of these silent Bengali women are not dead, but they anticipate death, as they do everything, with resignation. There is no dignity in their death as in the death of that proud and glorious beast (tiger), but only a little melancholy as in the settling of a puff of dust upon the earth. (120-21)

Nirode is unsettled by Monisha's "unprotected state of nerves." It makes him wary and off-hand as did his mother's attentions and Monisha's silent agony behind the barred windows of her house." (189) It is through Nikhil, a schoolboy that the novel drives home the lack of space in a joint family:

> So many uncles in this house, so many aunts and cousins. Everyone having guests and visitors, all coming and going. If I want to speak to them, my father says 'Go to your room and do your lessons.' If I go to my room and study, my mother comes and says 'why don't you come and pay your respects to them? I know nothing, then they complain I know nothing.' It is a bad system, this joint family, it makes it very hard for me to study and pass examinations. (162)

Monisha is a non-entity in the joint family. Her husband cares little for her and when she removes money from his pocket to spend on Nirode's treatment without telling him, she is almost branded a thief. Jiban instead of accepting her right to money, questions: 'why did you not tell them at once?' He said, 'why didn't you tell me before you took it?' (138) By suspecting her honesty, Jiban further alienates her.

The fragile romantic idealistic core of Monisha draws her perception of love from *Bhagvad Gita*—love without strings attached to it, a state which is too ideal to be realised in this selfish world:

> If only love existed that is not binding, that is free of rules, obligations, complicity and all stirrings of mind or conscience then—but there is no such love. It is not there in my relationship with Jiban, which is filled only by loneliness and a desperate urge to succeed, and once plunged me into the most çalamitous pleasures and pains, fears and regrets, and never again will it possess me. Nor is it there in my relationship with mother which is filled with an inbred and invalid sense of duty, of honour, of concern. (135-36)

In none of the relationships she had: husband, mother, brother could she seek unfettered space. Each of these drew her in symbiotic possessiveness that stifled her. Rabindra Nath Tagore could sense the reasons of dissonance in human relationship and his song offers an elegy to the sad end of several lives like Monisha's:

> Why did the flower fade?

I clutched it to my heart
in excess of feelings and crushed it

Why did the lamp go out?
I shielded it with my cloak
And it got no air. (1936:123)

She is like a tender sapling transplanted on to the soil and milieu that contrasted with the one for which it was meant, and her young life gets terminated in suicide.

VII

Amla, along with Monisha, represents the diverse facets of feminine lives. Their relationship to Nirode provides the novelist the scope to probe deeper into his psychic labyrinths. She has been drawn as comparatively a down-to-earth personality though she shares with Nirode and Monisha some of the family traits. She comes to Calcutta from Bombay trained as a commercial artist to join an advertisement firm. The typical reaction of middle-class society is expressed in comments she gets from no less a man than Nirode, a staunch opponent of commercial art, yet peddling fake antique pieces as genuine art and herein lies his hollowness and all his anger and indignation at society fall flat: "Commercial artist. Sounds too bloody awful for words. Poor old Amla, Do you really expect anything from a career stamped commercial?" (154) These are the words coming from the same Nirode who has no hesitation in selling a fake bronze depicting:

> Shiva and Parvati locked together in an upright embrace that pulsed with so grand a desire, so rich a satisfaction that soon the girls, too, looked away from that inscrutable smile on Shiva's face and the taut buttocks of Parvati who had turned her back on the world as she pressed upon her consort her purpose and her delight, inexplicable to both the girls. (147)

The statue was made by a dubious friend of Nirode "and buried underground for three weeks to give it the appearance of three centuries of age." (148) She meets Dharma, an artist friend of Nirode who is a painter in his own right. His daughter has eloped with her cousin and in order to escape humiliation, he has left

Calcutta and settled down in a suburb. Landscape is his main interest but association with Amla shifts his attention to portrait painting. Dharma seems to take interest in her not as a person, but as a model. Her young romantic disposition cannot help wondering how deep could he reach into her soul? Unless he knows the soul of the subject, how can he paint the portrait. Amla is initially attracted to Dharma but because of the opposition from Nirode and more so because of her own practical self, she realises that falling in love with a married man is of no consequence; it is a journey to a dead end. She withdraws herself from him. The infatuation dies down; she neither kills herself nor does she feel lost. For Dharma, Amla was not a living being, but merely a subject for painting: "He stared at her, but Amla knew instinctively it was not her face he was studying, but the collective face of society, the weak, amorphous, irresponsible face he hated so much." (227)

The narration proceeds with the reference to the elopement of Dharma's fifteen-year old daughter with her first cousin, "my sister's son, a boy who I had brought up as her brother." (228) The question that haunts Amla's mind is "What was it in society that he truly hated—the rules and restrictions that he verbally opposed, or their transgression that he secretly feared and loathed?" (228) Dharma, like Nirode, although in a different context, denounces the institution of marriage. Talking of his marital relationship, when Amla asks about his wife's sympathy with him or the daughter, he says, "Our relationship is not all so straightforward and pat, married relationships never are. There is the matter of loyalty, habit, complicity—things I couldn't talk to you about till you married and knew for yourself." (229)

Desai generalises diverse point of views to reveal alternative worldviews and also to dilute the nihilistic world of Nirode. The question of "choices" could also involve not surrendering to the dehumanising effect of metropolitan cities, there is still a way out, rather two ways out, one more easily intelligible and the other more mystifying, symbolic and esoteric. The first being rather a bland solution that a happy, mature middle-aged Professor Bose would rather subscribe to in accordance with his age and maturity: "My dear Nirode . . . one must make concessions—how else one can survive?" (18) Nirode's problem draws us deep into his unconscious self-tracing secret suppressed cause of his self-loathing to his ambivalence to the city/mother/woman—symbolic of the feminine principle. He is periodically flooded with the consciousness of his mother's feminine attraction: "still beautiful . . . and her beauty compelled him to embrace her," "the stately and precise figure" "he could not take his eyes-off her, he watched her, petrified, as she came up with her exact and measured walk straight towards him." (251) She is the one, who "stood out as a work of art in a crowded, stuffy gallery." (253) Nirode reminisces that as a small boy "he fawned at her feet, almost grovelling over her long white toes, while she fastened her ear-rings and glanced with the same smile of pride from his little bowed back to her reflection in the mirror." (252)

Nirode's relation in his growing years with his mother could not give him a sense of security that a highly sensitive boy needed. Trapped between a weak father and a disapproving, inconsistent self-centred mother, his sense of self-esteem and identity always remained threatened. The powerful, rich, beautiful mother writes poetic letters to her children. Her beauty and poetry however is soulless to her children with whom she could never connect in terms of nurturing and mothering. Nirode calls her she-cannibal. Monisha refuses to rely on her in her distress. Nirode realized her power in draining him of "blood and passion." The mother is seen as an emasculating force.

The narrative of memories, in snatches and fragments, hints at the motivation that makes Nirode pursue the antithesis between spirit and flesh. Spirit eludes him and flesh repulses him. The image of his mother's sexuality that once attracted him now repulses him as an adult. Perhaps his disturbed childhood alienated him from a very basic relationship, that could have continued to sustain and nurture his adult life. The memory of not being owned by his mother, drives him to retaliate by not owning her or the city of Calcutta or even the very principle of feminine/maternity—the Kali. If only he could transcend the dichotomy between sexuality and spirituality, he could see the city, the

Mother Kali and his own mother merged as the emblem of creation and destruction. Nirode is doomed to be locked up forever in his adolescent rage never seeking maturity of vision.

VIII

Cry, the Peacock and *Voices in the City* illumine the recesses of human psyche. Family situation forms the principal scenario in the stories in an atmosphere of impending sense of doom. What comes to the fore from the two narratives is the anti-thesis between the male and the female worlds. Both indict the patriarchal norms that look down upon and condemn passionate nature in women, while poise, self-possession and composure are applauded as virtues. Maya is a tormented woman, her desolation and secret grief are not acceptable in social terms. Desai literally connects the narrative with the feminine body. *Cry, the Peacock*, Maya's narrative, disintellectualizes the "notion of writing" by subtly undermining the most rarefied preoccupations of male writings: with Atman, Brahman or with other metaphysical abstractions as in Raja Rao. Monisha in *Voices in the City* writes the narrative of her disintegration holding the patriarchal authority culpable. Both she and Maya trapped in incompatible marital life are seen as unreliable, capricious in terms of the social norms. Desai makes us see through the unresolved conflicts, unadmitted desires, traumatic cultural past, when unsuccessfully pushed out of consciousness, reach the realm of unconscious and communicate obliquely. Maya's and Monisha's narratives in two different ways embody what Mary Jacobus proposed in a woman writing—that works within 'male discourse' but works ceaselessly to deconstruct it: to write what cannot be written (1979: 12-13).

Works Cited

Bande, Usha. 1988. *The Novels of Anita Desai: A Study in Character and Conflict*. New Delhi: Prestige.

Desai, Anita. 1963. *Cry, the Peacock* Delhi: Orient Paperbacks.

_____ 1965 . *Voices in the City*. Delhi: Orient Paperback.

Gorden, Lynden. 1984. *Virginia Woolf: A Writer's Life*. Oxford: O.U.P.
Iyengar, K.R.S. 1973. *Indian Writing in English*. New Delhi: Sterling.
Jena, Seema. 1989. *Voices and Vision of Anita Desai*. New Delhi: Ashish.
Jacobus, Mary. 1979. "The Difference of View." *Women's Writing and Writing about Women*. New York: Barnes & Noble.
Mortimer, Penelope. 1988. *Pumpkin Eater*. London: Penguin.
Singh, B.N. 1988. *Dictionary of Indian Philosophy*. Varanasi: Asha.
Tagore, Rabindra Nath. 1936. *The Gardener*. New Delhi: Rupa, 2002.
Tripathi, J.P. 1986. *The Mind and Art of Anita Desai*. Bareilly: Prakash.

Chapter III

The Novels of the 1970s: Journeys, Revelations and Impasse

The wider canvas of *Bye-Bye Blackbird* touches issues of nationalism and cosmopolitanism and describes cultural and cross-cultural encounters in the lives of three major characters, namely Adit, his British wife, Sara and his newly arrived friend from Calcutta, Dev. The following, *Where Shall We Go This Summer?* reveals a woman's urge for autonomy. In retreating to the Manori's island, Sita returns to the feminine-semiotic landscape—the security and comfort of the maternal womb. *Fire on the Mountain* makes 'fresh demands' on the readers, draws them to see the secret selves of the characters that remain repressed and unacknowledged in most feminine lives. In the stories of women struggling to cope with the sense of not belonging—memories and dreams, the culminating scene of breaking out of fire on the mountains symbolizes an act of angry subversion. The fire brings about an end to the world of make believe of Nanda, the total destruction of flora and fauna in the smouldering flames brings us to the awareness of 'impasse' that the sapped, desiccated lives are finally left with.

II

The poetic evocation of the milieu, the landscape and environs of London and rural England lend a sustained credibility to the narrative in *Bye-Bye, Blackbird.* Adit having a flat, a middle-rung job in a travel agency and a white compatible wife, in the early part of the novel seems content with his fascination with the white cultural mores and Desai astutely describes his chauvinistic pride in acquiring a white bride. "These English wives are quite manageable really, you know. Not as fierce as they look—very quiet and hardworking as long as you treat them right and roar at them regularly once or twice a week" (Desai 1971: 29). The memories of home remind him of "Nothing ever goes right at home—there is famine or flood, there is draught or epidemic always" (129). During his visits to India, "the laziness of the clerks, and the unpunctuality of the buses and trains, and the beggars and the flies and the stench and the boredom of it" (49) disgust him.

The growing interaction with the English culture brings about disillusionment and he recognizes a sense of uneasiness, difficult to handle in the city of London. Spurred by the Indo-Pak War of 1967, he decides to return back to India.

Visiting England makes the characters like Adit and Dev find themselves in closer confrontation with their host country in terms of colonizer-colonized relation as England and India have had a recent history of such relationship. Indian immigrants across different sections of society have varied experiences in England. The less sensitive ones coming under the category of "factory hands, colour no bar" do not bother about racial discrimination. They are very happy with their earning and their small world of Indian fraternity. It is the educated, refined and sensitive men like Adit and Dev who are troubled and offended by the overt discrimination of racism. The novel ends on a telling note. Dev goes to Waterloo Railway Station to see off the Sens and on his way back he catches a city bus and while

> buying his ticket he felt certain—and then not so certain—that he saw a glint of scorn in the conductor's eye, the abrupt way in which he handed him his ticket and then kept him waiting for his change. He wondered if the old lady beside whom he sat down did not clutch her handbag and lean away from him as though she suspected a smell. (230)

Sarah, the British wife of Adit Sen, figures as a character struggling against a set of very difficult circumstances. Dev and Adit encounter situations of racial discrimination but Sarah's estrangement is much more intricate. By marrying a non-white, she has broken the social code, and all the more so having married to an Indian, one from the country which was once a British colony. The narrative gives the hints of disparaging attitude of the English to Adit and Indians in general. Sarah is mocked, taunted and ridiculed by her colleagues and even small children studying in the school where she is a clerk. The portraits of exile, identity crises and loneliness, are drawn from Desai's personal experience. She says in an interview, "Of all my novels it is most rooted in experience and the least literary in derivation . . . the closest of all my books to actuality—practically every thing in it is drawn directly from my experience of living with Indian immigrants in London." (Ram 1977: 221) She also admits that this is "the only book I've written that is truly about the objective world, objectively observed characters hence the lightness of it." (*ibid.*) Desai's visits and stay in England and other European countries, her sense of history make her keenly aware of a variety of immigrant experiences.

A white woman's marriage to a brown/black Indian in the 1960s and 70s indeed has been an act of courage, but the subsequent sense of rejection is brought about because she allows others to control her identity and does not muster the emotional resilience to fight back or assert her independence. Her easy susceptibility reduces her to a "victim" position. She could not realize that nobody could "make you feel inferior without your consent." Desai describes her intense quick-ranging self-doubt:

> Who was she—Mrs. Sen who had been married in a red and gold Benares brocade *sari* one burning, bronzed day in September, or Mrs. Sen, the Head's Secretary, who sent out the bills and took in the cheques, kept order in the school and was known for her efficiency? Both these creatures were frauds, each had a large, shadowed element of charade about it. When she briskly dealt with letters and bills in her room under the stairs, she felt an imposter, but, equally, she was playing a part when she tapped her fingers to the Sitar Music on Adit's records or ground spices for a curry she did not care to eat. She had so little command over these two charades she played each day, one in the morning at the school and one in the evening at home, that she could not even tell with how much sincerity she played one role or the other. They were roles—and

> when she was not playing them, she was nobody. Her face was only a mask, her body only a costume. Where was Sarah? . . . She wondered if Sarah had any existence at all, and then she wondered, with great sadness, if she would ever be allowed to step off the stage, leave the theatre and enter the real world—whether English or Indian, she did not care, she wanted only its sincerity, its truth. (34-35)

Even school children have guts to taunt her, "hurry, hurry, Mrs. Scurry" simply because she had married an Indian and this is perverted social value that causes the individual's dilemma in society: "As she darted through their throng, they pretended not to notice her at all but, once she was across the road, she heard them scream, "hurry, hurry, Mrs. Scurry!" and "where's the fire, pussy cat?" (32) Sarah is not only apologetic, she avoids any personal question from her colleagues "breathing hard at having so narrowly escaped having to answer personal question. It would have wrecked her for the whole day to have to discuss Adit with Julia, with Miss Pimm." (36) But in spite of her avoidance and interactions she cannot help overhearing "Julia Sniff, as she left the room, 'If she's that ashamed of having an Indian husband, why did she go 'and marry him'?" (37)

The narrative closes before Sarah reaches India. She sails to India where her first baby is to come. Unlike the Manichean white England India's polycentric, liberalism makes her easily accepted by Adit's family in Calcutta. Adit Sen finds in her some characteristics of Bengali, "You are like a Bengali girl." He tells her, "Bengali women are like that—reserved, quiet. Maybe you were one in your previous life." (73) Adit tells Dev how he would be enjoying his holiday in Calcutta, "When I have a whole month of leave, saved up, I'll go. My mother will cook *hilsa* fish wrapped in banana leaves for me. My sister will dress Sarah in Sarees and gold ornaments. I'll lie in bed till ten every morning and sit up half the night listening to the Shehnai and Sitar." (48) Sarah must wear the wedding present sent to her by Adit's family on their wedding anniversary:

> And he chose for her a *Sari* that his sisters had once sent her . . . and the gold necklace . . . sent by his mother as a wedding present.

> It was the one his mother used to wear during the festive Puja season. (193)

She must now say good-bye to her past twenty-four years:

> She felt all the pangs of saying good bye to her past twenty-four years. Yet it would be a great relief, for she'd be delivered from the tension of charade, the double role that she had to play in England, and ultimately, whether for good or bad, "she would be allowed to step off the stage." (35)

Desai's keen analysis aptly captures the moments of ambivalence that constitute immigrant attitudes. The routinized display of racism has hardened Adit and he has learned to live with the fact of his racial inferiority, accustomed to being called a wog while Dev in private moments unleashes, "disconcerted, swung around to catch Adit's reaction, to catch a cue for his own, but Adit turned carelessly aside and pointed out something in a show window to Sarah, his shoulders in an elaborately nonchalant slope." (14) Adit simply ignores these remarks and advises the same to Dev: "It is best to ignore those who don't deserve one's notice," Adit said, "in the care-paced voice of one who has learnt it as a lesson." (16) Adit's resilience however gets under strain:

> Why had this happened? Mrs. Roscommon-James [his mother-in-law] had scolded him before, had shot maddening looks of pity at Sarah before. His arguments with Dev had been nothing new either, mere repetitions of things they had often said before, out of a sense of duty rather than antagonism. He could not tell himself. "My mother-in-law hates and despises me. Dev makes fun of the life I lead and the ideals I profess. Therefore I am angry. I am hurt." It was nothing so precise and definable. This was not the sole or even the main reason for his mood. This mood had begun to enter him, circulate within him and alter him during the drive out of London, through the Hampshire fields, had accompanied him through the dismal dinner and the night when Sarah had shut him out with a bang and a snap, from her childhood of one-eared pandas and large jigsaw puzzles . . . but moods of anxiety and abstract pain were new to him. Faced with one, he was unable to deal with it—he merely stood still and felt his leaden feet sink in as though in quicksands. (176)

Adit had been an anglophile earlier but gradually the phoniness of his whole situation descends upon him. He too, like Sarah, questions his real identity and can no 'longer contain stress: "His whole personality seemed to her to have cracked apart into an unbearable number of disjointed pieces, rattling together noisily and disharmoniously." (200) He tells Sarah: "Our lives here—they've been so unreal, don't you feel it? Little India in London. All our records and lamb curries and sing-songs, it's all so unreal. It has no reality at all, we just pretend all the time. . . . I've loved England more than you, I've often felt myself half-English, but it was only a pretence, Sally. Now it has to be the real thing. I must go." (204)

The firebrand, bitter, critical and at times cynical Dev who feels himself in no way inferior to the British intellectually, by the end of the novel, is tamed and all his outrage and criticism peters out.

> Somewhere, at some point that summer, England's green and gold fingers had let go of Adit and clutched at Dev instead. England had let Adit drop and fall away as if she had done with him or realised that he had done with her, and caught and enmeshed his friend Dev. It was as though this were an arbitrary act of England's, an abstract law to which Adit and Dev had quite unwittingly succumbed. (229)

The experiences of "exile," not belonging or being disowned, in *Bye-Bye Blackbird* impact Sarah more seriously than Dev and Adit who in their diasporic situation present in variation the common expatriate experiences. Sarah had not visualized before that she was choosing her isolation deliberately by marrying a foreigner that rendered her exile in her own land. Sarah's loneliness is not easy to penetrate. The causes could be multiple, not unequivocably communicated in the novel, but as a reader, one senses what it means to survive as a sensitive human being in a culture which values eurocentric norms of class, gender and race. As a woman, she is vulnerable in her chauvinistic white cultural mores, her marriage to Adit has made her doubly susceptible to social prejudice.

In Sarah's musings we discern nostalgic anxiety of a divided self:

> She had shed her name as she had shed her ancestry and identity, and she sat there, staring, as thought [sic] she watched them disappear. Or could only someone who knew her, knew of her background and her marriage, imagine this? Would a stranger have seen in her a lost maiden in search of her name. (31)

She avoided talking about her personal matters or any reference to her husband: "to discuss her Indian husband, would have forced her to parade like an impostor, to make claims to a life, an identity that she did not herself feel to be her own." (37) In London she wants to remain inconspicuous avoiding any manifestation of the fact of being married to an Indian, even while shopping for grocery, she would avoid a shop on Laurel Lane where the proprietor knows of her Indian husband, hence, she would go to the supermarket:

> She loved the supermarket. . . . The supermarket was a soothing place to her. Here she could buy her Patna rice and her pickles without acquiring the distinct personality these purchases would have marked her with, had she shopped them in one of those pleasant little shops at the end of Laurel Lane. . . . But inside the sparkling halls of the supermarket where walls of soap and cornflakes, hid her from strangers' eyes, she could be as eccentric, as individual as she pleased without being noticed by even a mouse. She walked out into the soft, muzzling rain with her packages, reassured to find herself an unidentifiable, unnoticed and therefore free person again. (38-39)

Dev reminds us of Nirode in *Voices in the City* except that, unlike Nirode, Dev adjusts himself and becomes one of the many Indian immigrants in London, who in spite of fretting and complaining hold on to immigrant status because of the mercenary interest His dystopic wishful thinking borne out of helplessness is rather naïve: "Let history turn the tables now. Let the Indian traders come to England. Let them take over the city. . . . Let all British women take to the graceful *sari* and all British men to the noble *dhoti*." (61-62)

II

Anita Desai's fourth novel *Where Shall We Go This Summer?* (1975) describes Sita's "rite of passage" but with a difference. The story moves around a family which consists of Raman, his wife Sita and four children and the fifth child which is yet to be born, still plays an important role in the story. The fifth pregnancy of Sita brings about the events in retrospection and also links the present with the past. Like many of her other heroines, Sita's unusual childhood plays an important role in shaping her personality. During the winters of 1947, Sita, then a young girl, lived in Manori island, where her father was supposed to be a legend. A freedom fighter and social worker, he was too busy to look after his children. She had had an insecure motherless deprived childhood, and yet she had enjoyed the flora and fauna of the island. After the death of her father, she was married to Raman, the son of her father's friend Deedar. Deedar had arranged this marriage more out of pity than for love. Raman is an ordinary man, financially well off, running a factory but he is too commonplace to meet the expectations of Sita. Initially Sita lives in Raman's joint family which is willing to "accept even such an outrageous outsider" like Sita. But because of Sita's haughty, supercilious, unadjusting nature, Raman decide to live separately with his family in a flat. He tries to make Sita happy but she is hard to please and she is always seething with anger, discontent, and apathy. When Sita becomes pregnant for the fifth time, it is an ordeal for her, and she does not want to deliver the child. Manori island seems to her the enchanted island of miracles and against the sane advice of Raman, she decides to go there, along with her two children Menaka and Karan during her advanced stage of pregnancy. On the island she expects for a miracle that never comes about. Her retreat to the island is symbolic of her regression to childhood. Here she renews contact with her past, fantasizing over her childhood and her father who was a god to the illiterate islanders. The children get annoyed and fed up with the primitive life on the island, Menaka asks her father to take them back to Bombay. Raman comes and takes the family away though Sita too goes telling herself: "Life had no periods, no stretches. If simply swirled around muddling and confusing; leading nowhere" (Desai, 1975: 155). B. Ramachandra Rao reads the novel as a dramatisation of "the conflict between two irreconcilable temperaments, of two diametrically opposed attitudes towards life. The tragedy in *Where Shall We Go This Summer?* arises out of the inability of the characters to connect the prose and the passion in their lives. They have lived only in fragments. The novel ends with a defeated and despondent Sita unable to rediscover the passion of life and deciding to accept the prose of life." (1977: 51, 60) Rao's opinion dogmatically endorses a patriarchal view of labelling Sita's condition in terms of "prose and passions." Naik however probes deeper:

> *Where Shall We Go This Summer?* (1975) marks a return to the autonomous world of inner reality. Sita, the main character here, appears to be a less morbid than Maya after four children. The cruelty and callousness of urban life stifle her and when she is with child again, she panics at the thought of bringing a new, fragile being into this harsh world and runs away to a small island, which has childhood association for her; but finally allows her husband to persuade her to return. The novel is tightly structured and the island is an evocative symbol of a lost paradise, but Sita's sudden capitulation at the end comes as an anti-climax. (1987: 242)

The return of Sita from unfettered but lost, illusory fanciful world to the appallingly mundane routinized rut in Bombay could by no stretch of imagination be seen as a journey from subnormalcy to normalcy. The novel invokes a sense of lost time: "All the yesterdays pass into nothingness." A sense of passing time, of experiences and people invest a sense of grim desolation to Sita's narrative. The tone suggesting the appalling power of time has been set at the beginning:

> a waste of ashes she saw, the cold remains of the bonfire her father had lit here to blaze. Ashes, white and waste. Dust lay as casually as sound on a beach, spider-webs spanned the corners of the unfurnished rooms like skeletal palm leaves. The odour was of bats and mildew, and silence boomed like the silence of undersea caves. It

> had no air of providing shelter from the sea or beach—it was as much a natural part of Them as an abandoned shell or lump of twisted driftwood. (28)

Jasbir Jain sees a polarized world in the novel and endeavours to come to terms with Sita's situation:

> There is a Rousseaustic opposition between the world of island and the city, but this opposition is not allowed to remain unquestioned. The contrast is underlined, the different worlds are demarcated, and the focus shifted from outside to inside, from the surroundings to human relationships and from the collective to the general. Sita is perhaps, at heart, an islander. (1987: 86)

Her deep obsession with nature is the novelist's way of contrasting the urban, artificial with the natural world but this apparent contrast is intersected with heavy irony.

The island however in Sita's retrospection is no longer an innocence suggesting Prospero's island in *The Tempest*. It begins to ingrain many more ironic connotations. Sita would want this to be her sanctum sanctorum, she would like to be a part of this world, the daughter of the mother earth, *Prakriti Putri* protected from the dubious, vicious world but the contact with the ambiguities of her relation with the past, "the other side" of story, the half-truths expanding into uneasy facts make the nature of her journey loaded with irony. As readers we discern a perennial shadow of loneliness afflicting her since the times of her drifting, derelict childhood to being a misfit in her adulthood.

Sita represents the rebellion against the vegetable existence of women in Raman's family. Her return, therefore, is not her acceptance nor does it show growth, ripeness; it is rather a sad compromise with the harsh facts of life which offers no alternatives to conventional feminine existence. While the novel echoes Katherine Anne Porter's long short story "The Cracked Looking Glass," we may sense a strong presence of Virginia Woolf's *To the Lighthouse* in the novel. The novel reverberates with metaphors of birds. As in *Cry, the Peacock*, Sita sees herself as a wounded eagle. The bird image makes us see her as a trapped eagle whose wings are clipped. She is also compared with the foreign tourist with whom she identifies because like her she is so vulnerable. Her journey into Manori island is a spiritual rite of passage—passage into the past—in retrospection now she can make sense of her past with keener insight and maturity. This sojourn-hibernation, despite being ephemeral and short lived, gives her the incentive to "go on" in the process of living; let tomorrow pass into yesterdays.

In the memory-narrative, Sita reminisces, when she is told that her mother had run away to Benares, she refuses to believe it and wonders, "Ran away? And left us? . . . Your stories, Jiban," she shouted. "What stories you tell?" with the initial shock and bewilderment as to "why had she left her husband whom they called a second Gandhi?" (86) It is painful for her to accept reality:

> Sita preferred to accept that. Mother alive and well in a place no further than Benares would have been an idea she could not cope with, used to being without one. Life seemed complete, full, without her, there was no reason for her to exist. Sita had imagined she came into this world motherless—and the world was crowded enough. . . . She belonged, if to any one, to this whole society that existed at that particular point in history—like a lamb does to its flock and saw no reason why she should belong to one family alone. As she was not sent to school, she only came in contact with other families like her own and life seemed normal. She could not remember wanting or waiting for her mother. (84-85)

Brought up by her father, he would be too busy, either in jail or going underground or busy in meetings. Drifting and derelict, volatile child would collect discarded garlands and played with the tinsel till she fell asleep against a bolster and was carried away to someone's house to sleep—always a different someone, it scarcely mattered which one." (85) Even though she did not miss her mother as a child, she was deprived of her father's soothing presence.

Sita's awe of her father's persona recollected in the roles of a saviour, patriot, healer, magician, and social emancipator imbues his character with mystique. In rapidly shifting focus, the narrative presents his relation with his stepdaughter Rekha ambiguously, hinting at his incestual inclination. The apparent attachment between the two would give away hints of physical intimacy, surreptitious meeting of eyes make Sita jealous of Rekha specially after Jiban tells her that Rekha is her step-sister and, there is no physical similarity between them. This knowledge agitates her:

> but his words had dropped on her skin like acid and she felt them burn whenever she caught an exchange of that heavy-lidded look between father and the daughter, or his arms in its fine white sleeve lie fondlingly across her round shoulders. (79)

Like the mysterious story of her mother's disappearance, relationship between Rekha and her father in retrospection no longer remains a mystery. The adult Sita reaches an awareness of the past. The authorial comment illumines Sita's lonely adolescence:

> It was one more relationship that had to remain shrouded, a ghost in her life, because of the impossibility of talk between her and her father. . . . She told herself she could never approach him to ask of such private and, somehow, secret matters. As an adult, later, she asked herself, had there been no opportunity ever of talking alone to him? Ah! She remembered, with an instinctive shrinking from the shock and the pain, a few strange moments, still unexplained. . . . There had been other occasions—a few . . . but she shrank away from them, shutting them away in the dark. They had all been wordless and agitated by the queerest, the most horrible sensations. Only once she had come close, very close, to asking. (79-80)

A many-faceted man, he is also a charlatan giving glittering drugs to the villagers by mixing gold and precious stones. We are not sure about his motive. Once when Deedar, his friend who would later become Sita's father-in-law, asked about this hoax, he says it is a matter of faith. He puts a rational question, "You studied Chemistry at school with me! Don't tell me you believe pearls and gold have therapeutic value?" He replies:

> "No," came the soft, bubbling reply. . . . "No student of Chemistry can believe that. Any one who has seen as much of life as I have, can't believe that. But what have these islanders seen? Nothing. . . . *Their* faith has never been shaken. And do you deny the therapeutic

> value of faith? They believe gold is the best thing on earth—best because most valuable. So why not add a little to these powders. . . . They believe it does them good and then it really does. (82)

He is treated like a demigod by the islanders during his life time and even after his death, as shown in the last pages of the novel through the mouth of minor characters like Moses and Jamila, who serve like the Chorus in the novel, like the rustics in Hardy's novels. In Jamila's eyes Sita does not have even an iota of her father's grand personality as Jamila says: "'Not like him. . . . She—she looks plain. A plain woman. No body. Not like her father. That was a man,' she smacked her lips appreciatively." (156) She broods over him and even as a child she had an ambivalent attitude towards him. There was no communication between them and so no human relationship. As a child she had observed him surrounded by his *chelas* and venerated by women prostrating themselves at his feet. We do not know whether the islanders were cured by coincidence or by their faith in him. Sita herself found as a child that, whatever the villagers attributed to father was not true, for example, the well that was dug on the island was declared to have sweet water by the islanders, whereas Sita found it hard water. In some respect Sita's father reminds us of Gautama's mother in *Cry, the Peacock* who could be put on a pedestal and worshipped but there could be no possibility of human intimacy with her: "The gods might one day erect a monument to her, though human beings would not." (158)

V

Sita would like to be eternally housed in her childhood, that even in her childhood was a distant dream. Conjugal relation in adult life, therefore to her is distasteful: "They are nothing—nothing but appetite and sex. Only food, sex and money matter. Animals." (47) When Raman says, "I thought you liked animals," she bursts out: "My pet animals—or wild animals in the forest, yes. But these are neither: they are like pariahs you see in the streets, hanging about drains and dustbins, waiting to pounce and kill and eat." (47) The loathing for violent physical contact peeps through these highly suggestive outbursts. It is ironical that she is tender to animals, even pathologically tender, is tender to animals, even pathologically tender, but she has no tenderness or affection towards her children, husband and her in-laws. And even then, she feels that she is betrayed by her children and husband. An example of her pathological tenderness can be seen in the episode of the wounded eagle being killed by the crows. Menaka's trampling on tender buds or tearing off the paintings that she did not like get on Sita's nerves. She wants her family members to share her perception of life and when they do not, she feels let down. Menaka's character is a clear contrast to hers. She finds her mother theatrical and insufferable, for she is a practical girl who finds no charm in the island with its dirt and poverty. Sita's hypersensitivity makes her a psychological case, for she cannot stand the humdrum life of the usual noises and quarrels natural among children. She cannot even read the newspaper which abounds in news of violence, destruction and death:

> her husband casually handed her the newspaper on his way out to office. They all hammered at her with cruel fists—the fallen blocks—the torn watercolours, the headlines about the war in Vietnam, the photograph of a woman weeping over a small grave, another of a crowd outside a Rhodesian jail; articles about the perfidy of Pakistan . . . they were hand-grenades all, hurled at her frail goldfish-bowl belly and instinctively she laid her hands over it, feeling the child there play like some soft-fleshed fish in a bowl of warm sea-water . . . frightened, certain now that civilization had been created by the godlike efforts of the few, in the face of a constant, timeless war of destruction that had begun with time and was now roaring around her, battering her and her fish-foetus so that survival seemed hopeless. How could civilization survive, how could the child?`How could she hold them whole and pure and unimpeached in the midst of this bloodshed? They would surely be wounded, fall and die. (55-56)

Raman's advice to her is sane and sensible: "But you're not leaving for such small incidents, Sita? They occur in everyone's life, all the time. If you are an adult, you know how to cope with them—they are only *small* incidents." (37)

Most stereotypical concept of femininity and maternity is subjected to re-vision in Sita's story. "She hated the sight of their red faces, dripping, their chopped hair, sticking in clumps with sweat." But the phenomenon of birth is an act of creation and also an act of mystery. The poem whose line she has been trying to remember for long also suggests it. It is a poem by D.H. Lawrence which along with other things suggests the secrecy of the act of giving birth, especially the last three lines:

> Nay, even the slumbrous egg as it labours under the shell
> Patiently to divide and sub-divide,
> Asks to be hidden, and wishes nothing to tell.

Numerous critics have chosen to see Sita from Raman's point of view. They perceive Raman as a stolid, rational man, earning his livelihood, trying to discharge his duties to the best of his ability, but looks down upon Sita and perceives her as a muddled up philosopher, supercilious, unsociable, mentally living in the world of past, escaping from her duty both as mother and as wife. Neither attached to her husband nor to her children, she fails to play her social role of wife and mother. The novelist however in her depiction exposes another face of feminine desire, without being judgemental about it. The in-depth analysis of Sita's growth explains why she refuses to give birth to a child in a world not fit to receive the child. Obviously Sita represents the category of men and women with whom Desai empathizes, whose hearts cry out 'the great No,' who fight the currents and struggle against it, they know what the demands are and what it costs to meet them." (Dalmia, 1997). The rejection of the given roles constitutes the mystique of Desai's women, "She had cried out her great "No," but now the time had come for her epitaph to be written." (137)

VI

Fire on the Mountain, awarded the Sahitya Akademi and also the Royal Society Award, brought Desai into limelight. The novel reveals a new type of aesthetic evolution in Desai's art. Darshan Singh Maini plays a noteworthy compliment to the novelist in these words: "I trust this is probably Anita Desai's nearest brush with the Jamesian nouvelle, a form which the Master

[Henry James] adored for its blessed deep breathing economy" (1977: 132).

Nanda Kaul, the widow of a Vice-Chancellor, is compelled both by choice and circumstances to live in a secluded old bungalow 'Carignano' in Kasauli, fiercely guarding her seclusion and privacy. But her insulated self-consciously impervious life is disturbed by the arrival of her great-granddaughter Raka, a girl of seven or eight years, introvert, sensitive and, like Nanda, very much confined to her own self, resenting any intimacy with her *Nani*, Nanda. She busies herself rambling through deserted locale of hills and gorges. It is the nature's expanse of desolation that draws her:

> It was the ravaged, destroyed and barren spaces in Kasauli that drew her: the ravine where yellow snakes slept under grey rocks and agaves growing out of the dust and rubble, the skeletal pines that rattled in the wind, the wind-levelled hill-tops and the seared remains of the safe, cosy, civilized world in which Raka had no part and to which she owed no attachment. (Desai 1977: 91)

She is specially attracted towards a burnt house and is preoccupied with the idea of a forest fire. A childhood friend of Nanda, Ila Das, a Welfare Officer, dedicated to social reforms has fallen on bad days. She comes for tea with Nanda one afternoon. They have long chat about their early days, her experiences as a social worker and also Nanda's life as the Vice-Chancellor's wife.

On her way back when it was getting dark, near the village Preet Singh, an old man, angered by Ila Das's opposition to the child marriage, waited for her in ambush and brutally assaulted, raped and killed her: "Crushed back, crushed down into the earth, she lay raped, broken still and finished. Now it was dark" (143). This is the punishment brought up by the androcentric social norms which see Ila as the transgressor of the existing social order—the child marriage. Cixous rightly recalls history in her comment that women who are seen as the threat to the male system "are decapitated, their tongues are cut off . . . a woman who disturbs is nothing but disturbance" (1981: 49). Ila's voice challenges, disturbs, amuses and irritates the dominant culture. It is only through violence that she could be silenced. Nanda gets a phone-call about the outrage by the Police Inspector. She is shaken by the shocking news of her friend's violent rape and death. She is in a state of collapse when Raka announces that she has set the forest on fire.

VII

Much more than Nanda Kaul's choice of seclusion, what seems most intriguing in the novel is the portrayal of Raka as a recluse. It is obviously in Raka that the novel excavates the roots of several psychological disorders afflicting women. Raka's interiority therefore needs to be visualized with greater sensitivity. Desai gives us the subtle suggestions:

> If Nanda Kaul was a recluse out of vengeance for a long life of duty and obligation, her great granddaughter was a recluse by nature, by instinct. She had not arrived at this condition by a long route of rejection and sacrifice—she was borne to it, simply. (48)

Though Raka has not been through a "long route of rejection and sacrifice," unlike her grandmother, she has nonetheless been a witness to the abject degradation of her mother:

> Somewhere behind them, behind it all, has her father, home from a party, stumbling and crashing through the curtains of night, his mouth opening to let out a flood of rotten stench, beating at her mother with hammers and fists of abuse—harsh, filthy abuse that made Raka cower under her bedclothes and wet the mattresses in fright, feeling the stream of urine warm and weakening between her legs like a stream of blood and her mother lay down on the floor and shut her eyes and wept. (71-72)

Raka, like an animal chased, would flee these scenes, sobbing, "Hate them—Hate them." (71) Nanda Kaul secretly suffered the betrayal and infidelities of her husband. The psychology of perennial victimhood afflicted her consciousness to the extent that she developed apathy and detachment even to her own children. To her, the mountains, wilderness, flora and fauna of Kasauli serve as the substitute of human society. To both Nanda and Raka the landscape offers a refuge. Nanda hopes for tranquillity—liberty from the history of pain that she had had. She would not allow the past grief of her life to surface and yet the wounds, the bruises remain dormant, not receptive to healing as Emily Dickinson says (Oliver 1998: 331) :

> They never did assuage;
> Time never did assuage,
> An actual suffering strengthens,
> As sinews do, with age.
> Time is a test of trouble,
> But not a remedy
> If such it prove, it prove too
> There was no malady

Nanda had no wish to "be drawn into a child's world again—real or imaginary it was bound to betray" (45). But here is a child who prefers "to stand apart," to be distant and elusive. The child refuses to be drawn by Nanda's stories. Her absence as much as her arrival is disquieting "Raka's genius, Raka's demon. It disturbed." (64) Raka's indifference, her complete independence attracts Nanda, it is what she desires for herself. With Raka, Nanda senses uncanny affinity. Raka may not be responding to her, but she sees her as her doppelganger. "You are more like me than any of my children or grandchildren. You are exactly like me, Raka." (64) It is Raka who stirs in her after all these years a desire to be loved. Her husband's adulterous affair, her children's selfish demands, her busy socializing as a Vice-Chancellor's wife, nothing had been able to shake her as profoundly as Raka's rejection of her. The ending of the novel with Ila Das's brutal murder, Nanda's desire to be free from bondage, almost an existentialist will to rise above human obligations, fails.

The early childhood years of Raka expose her to inexplicable forms of violence and terrible suffering. Raka's detachment—her rejection of the adult world and its delusions testifies to an intensely powerful femininity in a strange way impervious to male dominance. The extremities of cruelty meted out to herself and her mother makes her resentful of any pre-cast notion of identity. She identifies with the monstrous, enigmatic alien dark interiority of wilderness and in her as if she exorcises a threatening power of nature, she would not choose to be a frozen angel but would rather be a wrathful monster woman who would reject all roles that domesticate her. Unable to identify with the adult world, she would not "socialize" with the children of her age. Her "long illness" acquitted her of any need to do so. Nothing could draw Raka to Nanda and least of all her stories of adventure laced with fantasy. The conversation between Ila Das and Nanda—the nostalgic recollection of their past repulses Raka:.

> It seemed the old ladies were going to play, all afternoon, that game of old age—that reconstructing, block by gilded block, of the castle of childhood, so ramshackle and precarious, and of stuffing it with that dolls' house furniture. . . . She very much wanted to eat her tea, but it seemed she would have to pay for it. (116-17)

Nanda admits the lies she had told Raka, the persona she had assumed, her relation to her husband, her role as a perfect hostess and events about her children.

> She had lied to Raka, lied about everything. Her father had never been to Tibet—he had bought the little Buddha from a travelling peddler. They had not had bears and leopards in their home, nothing but overfed dogs and bad-tempered parrots. Nor had her husband loved and cherished her and kept her like a queen—he had only done enough to keep her quiet while he carried on a life long affair with Miss David, the mathematics mistress, whom he had not married because she was a Christian but whom he had loved, all his life loved. And her children—the children were all alien to her nature. She neither understood nor loved them. She did not live here alone by choice—she lived here alone because that was what she was forced to do, reduced to doing. All those graces and glories with which she had tried to captivate Raka were only a fabrication: they helped her to sleep at night, they were tranquillizers, pills. She had lied to Raka. And Ila had lied, too. Ila, too, had lied, had tried. (145)

A deep sense of shame overwhelms Nanda; in grotesque and bizarre images, Desai captures the gothicized gorges and grooves of Nanda's wounded psyche.

> Looking down, over all those years she had survived and borne, she saw them, not bare and shining as the plains below but like the gorge, cluttered, choked and blackened with the heads of children and grand-children, servants and guests, all restlessly surging, clamouring about her. . . . She thought of her sons and daughters of her confinements, some in great discomfort at home and others at the small filthy missionary-run hospital in the bazaar, . . . She seemed to hear poignant shrieks from the canna beds in the garden—a child had tumbled off the swing, another had been stung by a wasp, a third slapped by the fourth—and gone out on the veranda to see them come wailing up the steps with cut lips, bruised knees, broken teeth and tears, and bent over them with that still, ironic *bow to duty that no one had noticed or defined.* (17-19)

Desai exposes her readers to the dim lit corridors of feminine lives, calling into question quite a few stereotypes. Her allegiance to the subjective truths bring to the fore an awareness that looking after a family could be cumbersome and demanding as every housewife knows too well. Nanda's situation is more pathetic because engagement—fake or real with her family has been most unrewarding to her. She does not get love from her husband. Always seething within even though she may appear to be happy—a regal woman, respected by the wives and daughters of the lecturers and professors over whom her husband ruled: "Isn't she splendid? Isn't she like a queen? Really, the Vice-Chancellor is lucky to have a wife who can run everything as she does." (18) In performing her social roles of the mother and perfect hostess, she is made to live several divided selves. While discharging her filial duty she may have annihilated herself but who bothers about it, hence her statement, "duty that no one had noticed or defined." She is torn asunder between her two roles—social role of the Vice-Chancellor's wife and biological role of a mother. Women are maternal, but the bedrock of woman's life is happy marital life which is possible only with a considerate, understanding, loving husband. Ironically in the process of playing a perfect host and rearing children, her emotional being is constantly wounded and is reduced to a charred tree-stump, an image that recurs in the novel. It is Nanda who invests with nature her own desolation, her own fragmentation and inexorable estrangement.

The narrative catches the phantasmagoria of profoundly disturbed states of mind, of brooding, precocious childhood, the loneliness of growing years, and the impact of abused infancy. Raka rejects the idea of going to school, "She could only shake her head dumbly, hating this craftiness, rejecting outright the very thought of school, of hostels, of discipline, order and obedience." (59) Nanda is upset by Raka's secretiveness and unsharing nature. She is complete in herself, not needing any company. The little contact that she has with Ram Lal is only to satisfy her curiosity as shown in her questioning about the laboratory and *Churail*. Nanda thinks: "Raka's genius. Raka's daemon. It disturbed." (64) Raka detests being watched or probed: "She hated her great-grandmother intently watching her ascent." (64) In the lawless wilderness of Kasauli, she finds a source of drive and inspiration. Within this landscape she makes a genuine, unfettered contact with herself. Fire draws Raka, when she sees it for the first time: "Shivers ran through her, zig-zag, leaving streams of sweat in their wake" (74). During that night she keeps "getting out of bed and coming barefoot into the drawing-room to look out of the window and see the fire spread" (75).

A burnt house that she visits frequently attracts her. Her secret passion and intensity make people see her as crazy: "The caretaker of the burnt house . . . saw her running. 'The crazy one,' he muttered. 'The crazy one from Carignano.'" (91) Raka's wilderness, freedom and precocity have driven readers to see in her traces of Pearl in *The Scarlet Letter* and Beatrice in Hawthorne's "Rappaccini's Daughter." The psychological motivation that Desai gives her character reveals conspicuous affinity with Henry James' "What Marie Knew" and Katherine Anne Porter's "Downward Path to Wisdom": both stories of initiation and experience drive home the grim consequences of a child's exposure to the viciousness and deceit of the adult world. Her unsociability, her ease and fearlessness with nature make her unique, different from normal children which is summed up succinctly, "The child who never played games." (121) She is not at all perturbed by dangers that may be lurking in wilderness, the mad jackals against whom Ram Lal çautions her. She walks down to the club in the moonlit night without any fear, some thing unnatural for a girl of her age. Shanta Krishnaswamy rightly observes that her "traumatic childhood has hardened her into a hard little core of solitary self-sufficiency and now recovering from a bout of typhoid, her spirit is defiant enough" (1982 262). She seems to be perfectly at ease in the wilderness and she would pass her days moving around the hills and when she would come home, "She would return with her brown legs scratched, her knees bruised, sucking a finger stung by nettles, her hair brown under a layer of dust, her eyes very still and thoughtful as though she had visited strange lands and seen fantastic, improbable things that lingered in the mind." (46) The narrative proceeds further with a prophetic tone, anticipating the culmination of the dormant fiery storm into`visible-livefire:

> This hill with its one destroyed house and one unbuilt one, on the ridge under the fire-singed pines, appealed to Raka with the strength of a strong sea-current—pulling, dragging. There was something about it—illegitimate, uncompromising and lawless—that made her tingle. The scene of devastation and failure somehow drew her, inspired her.
>
> Not so the nurseries and bedrooms of her infancy, with their sickly sweet smells of illness, sadness, drink, medication, milk and tension. Not so the clubs and parks of the cities in which she had lived but to which no one had given her the necessary pass, the key . . . the safe, cosy, civilized world in which Raka had no part and to which she owed no attachment. (90-91)

Nanda seems to have taken the persona of a prophet of doom, her proximity fails to provide Raka with the expected rejuvenation. Raka's private fantasies and hallucination, unlike the adolescent protagonists of conventional "innocence and experience tales" do not help her build up resistance or imaginative "counter-world" or some moments of positive illuminations. Relations have subjugated both of them, threatened them with the prospects of victimization. In the sinister memories that pursue them—the history of long drawn attrition—they are forever tied to the bizarre nerve-wrecking images of patriarchal outrage and betrayal. The novel ends up as a damning critique of patriarchy.

References

Cixous, Helen. 1981. "Castration or Decapitation?" Trans. Annette Kuhn. *Sign* 7, 1.

Dalmia, Yashodhara. 29 April 1997. "Anita Desai: An Interview." *Times of India*.

Desai, Anita, 1971. *Bye-Bye Blackbird*. New Delhi: Vision (1985).

_______. 1975. *Where Shall We Go This Summer?* New Delhi: Orient Paperbacks (1985).

_______. 1977 *Fire on the Mountain*. New Delhi: Allied (1985).

Jain, Jasbir, 1987. *Stairs to the Attic: The Novels of Anita Desai*. Jaipur: Printwell.

Jena, Seema. 1989. *Voice and Vision of Anita Desai*. New Delhi: Ashish.

Krishnaswamy, Shanta. 1982. "Anita Desai—The Sexist Nature of Sanity." *The Women in Indian Fiction in English*. New Delhi: Ashish.

Maini, Darshan Singh. 1984. *Perspectives on Anita Desai*, ed. Ramesh K. Srivastava. Ghaziabad: Vimal.

Oliver, S. Egbert. 1998. *Emily Dickinson: An Anthology of American Literature*. New Delhi: Eurasia Publishing House.

Ram, Atma. 1977. "An Interview with Anita Desai," *The World Literature Written in English*, Vol. XVI, No. 1.

Chapter IV

The Novels of the 1980s: The Rupture of Time Warp

In *Clear Light of Day* Anita Desai presents her principal protagonist, Bim's life—her ways of coping with her shared past and personal past. The narrative unfolds the saga of a family, placing Bim, Tara, Raja, Baba, Mira Masi within the specific historic time. Bim and Tara have witnessed India's partition and independence from the colonial rule. The before and after of 1947 fraught with cultural and political anxieties impact the growth of the two characters. The narrative of retrieving the past might not be accurately consistent with historical authenticity, it is however the "truthful consciousness of oneself, one's character and nature" as Desai puts it in an interview (Uniyal 2000: 254) which forms the core of the novel and makes it immensely readable. Bim lives multiple realities. Using technique of uncoiling memories, the narrative blends memory with imagination to describe the lives of those who experience the pain of loss, dislocation; those, who have lived deeply and sensitively. The following novel, *In Custody* testifies to Desai's astonishingly varied range of awareness of men and women from vastly different background. Her grip on the ordinary, commonplace, even lumpen realities of an ineffectual small town college lecturer, Deven and his failures both in his social and domestic life is as tensile as her shrewd knowledge of the inner, sordid, mean-spirited world of the Urdu Poet, Nur. Desai may not be a political novelist but her immense empathy with the insulted and injured, her identification with the travails of mankind trapped in the contingent processes of history and politics is amply demonstrated in the novel, *Baumgartner's Bombay*. The displaced, diasporic consciousness of Hugo Baumgartner strikes in us cords of compassion for those who have had different racial and political history—who suffer destitution and deprivation in their craving for love and understanding.

II

Covering the childhood, adolescence, youth and the ageing of the Das children and coming down to modern India in the late Sixties, much of the action described in the novel *Clear Light of Day* belongs to the past. The present incorporates the major event of the marriage of Raja's daughter. Tara has come from Washington with her diplomat husband Bakul to attend the marriage. As the story progresses, we have a series of episodes which explore diverse aspects of the novel. The uncaring parents of Bim died when she was hardly out of her teens and she had to shoulder the responsibilities of the family. She is one of the few characters who faces the challenges of life and performs the male role as the head of the family. This is because Raja has escaped responsibility and gone to Hyderabad to live with his landlord Hyder Ali. He later marries Hyder Ali's only daughter Benazir and lives with his in-laws. He is a *Ghar-Janwai* (a man living at the in-law's house). Tara is married to Bakul and after the death of Mira *Masi*, only Bim and Baba, her mentally retarded younger brother, are left to live in the house.

Desai intended the novel as a record of the passage of time and it grows accordingly as a four dimensional piece on "how a family's life moves backwards and forwards in a period of time. The novel is about time as a destroyer, as a preserver and about what the bondage of time does to people, trying to tunnel under the mundane surface of domesticity." (*India Today* 1980: 142) In another interview also she has spoken about the significance of time "as palpable an existence as the spatial world perceived by the five senses." (Srivastava 1984: 224-25) Memory which is an aspect of time is signified by the epigraph of the novel which is from a poem by Emily Dickinson: "Memory is a strange bell—/Jubilee and knell." Elaborating on the significance and the part played by time, she says,

> What I have tried to prove is that although time appears to damage, destroy and extinguish one finds instead that nothing is lost, nothing comes to an end, but the spiral of life leads as much upwards as downwards and is in perpetual circular motion, both the past and the future existing always in time present. (Srivastava 1984: 224-25)

In Bim's musings, one gathers the story of Raja. Raja's devotion to Hyder Ali family is motivated by the glitter and glamour of Hyder Ali's house compared to which his own house was lustreless: "He felt there could be no house as dismal as his own, as dusty and grimy and uncharming." (Desai 1980: 49) Hyder Ali is not only his ideal but in a way also a veritable father substitute. The novel makes no suggestion that by marrying a Muslim he suffered social ostracism. Tara does not sever her relationship with Raja. Bim's estrangement from Raja however is not caused by his marrying a Muslim, but by his neglect and coldness to the family.

Bim rereads Raja's letter to her that says that as he has inherited properties after Hyder Ali's death, she can continue to live in the old house on the same rent. This makes her recognize the fact that to Raja she is more a tenant than a sister. Whatever longing for affection she expects from her brother, meets with a rude jolt. She subjects herself to desolation and grief in reading the letter frequently. When Tara visits her, Bim and she share their childhood memories. The long convoluted journey into the past of Bim probes the dismal prospects of choices available to women in the middle of the 20th century. Refusing to see Bim as a "new woman," Desai wryly observes: "Women have been committed to responsibilities for centuries and a great many older women in the past generation were very courageous and strong, had great achievement." (Uniyal 2000: 251)

The unhappy, frustrated, sexually unfulfilled and sometimes neurotic women of Desai's other stories seem to be replaced by a woman who has evolved her individuality. Mundane norm of happiness is not her objective. She has invested her life with values. The novel indeed represents a great leap forward in its depiction of a woman outgrowing the straitjacketing that the domestic and social constraints bring about. Unlike Maya in *Cry, the Peacock*, Bim does not recede into narcissistic imagination. She rather attains a spiritually and emotionally fulfilling sense of life developing understanding towards it. Indeed Bim's character grows in spite of adversity, lovelessness and betrayal. Commitment to the deprived, orphaned, love-lorn lends meaning to her being. The delicately drawn relationship of Bim and Mira Masi or Bim and Baba form intersecting tales, recalling William Faulkner's range of human compassion, affinities and mysterious resources of authentic human urge to connect with persons of different histories in humility and love.

III

It is Mira Masi who nurtures Das children during the period of their growth. Identified initially as a poor distant relative of Mrs. Das, she has come to Delhi to help the family during the last confinement of Mrs. Das. She brings with her a "new season in their lives, a season of presents, of green mangoes and companionship" (105). She performs multiple roles. Her deprivation as an adolescent, virgin widow in a perversely misogynist family subjected her to oppression and torture of the most abject kind. She sought neither love nor assurance. Treated periodically as a "useless slave," or as a "parasite" she is finally "turned out." In Das household she thinks she is needed:

> They crowded about her so that they formed a ring, a protective railing about her. Now no one could approach, no threat, no menace. (111)

Mira Masi instinctively feels assured for the first time in her life. She may be a non-entity with neither any influence nor authority; but for the Das children she is a mother-substitute, especially for Tara and Baba. After her arrival in the Das family there is a perceptible change in the house. The children have found in her a playmate and one from whom they could draw emotional sustenance. Tara being the youngest is very attached to her. When she reaches Delhi for the first time, she brings small presents for all the children: "She drew out the things she had been making for them ever since she had received their mother's summons—there were paper hats trimmed with parrot feathers, little slippers of felt and velvet for Tara's dolls, a scrap book of wedding and birthday cards for Bim, lions and giraffes made out of sticks and straw for Raja." (104) Bim's own mother never had time nor inclination to devote her life to the children. She was always busy playing cards or visiting the club with her husband. Almost always sick she was also a diabetic. The children were always forced to maintain a distance from the parents.

In this household, Mira Masi finds the scope to channel her maternal instincts. In feeding them, rearing them, supporting them, she becomes an indispensable mother figure:

> They wrapped themselves around her, smothering her in leaves and flawns. She laughed at the profusion, the beauty of a little grove that was the whole forest to her, the whole world. They sucked her dry of sustenance, she would give in without any sacrifice of will—it seemed in keeping with nature to do so. . . . She was the tree, she was the soil, she was the earth. She gives without asking or expecting in return: "Touching them watching them." (111)

In drawing her in the images of mother earth, Desai reveals abundance of maternal principle in the lives of unloved, unfulfilled women. And yet, could Mira Masi stop living in memories? The early experiences of being heckled, insulted and silted rebound on her with relentless impact.

Advancing age however drives her to derangement, realm of delusion in her old age. She loses control over herself, tears out her clothes to`the embarrassment of Bim. Her long suppressed unfulfilled self surfaces. In her state of delusion she becomes obsessed with the images of "the hidden scummy pool in which the bride-like cow they had once had had drowned." (99) In such a state it is only Bim who could understand and empathize. The "bride like cow" is Mira Masi, the childbride, withered and wasted with the demise of her young husband.

IV

Bim is shown growing as prematurely older with gray wisps of hair. In the backward and forward movement of the story, we encounter the cheerless years of her life as a schoolteacher living alone with Baba in the decaying house. Long years spent in taking care of the family, nursing Baba and senile Mira *Masi*, seem to have dried up the spring of love in her heart. When Tara and Bakul visit her, she tends to be in sour moods, always irritable and bitter. When Bakul proposed marriage to Tara years ago seeking Bim's approval, she says: "I don't think you need to ask any one—except Tara. Modern times. Modern India. Independent India" (81). Bim had begun to gray in her youth, Bakul cracks a joke: "I'll have to buy you a bottle of Blacko for your hair, Bim. . . . I won't have you coming gray-haired to my wedding. Can't have such an elderly sister-in-law, I can't." (81) Though she is tall and graceful, more appealing than Tara, the latter draws men. Not that she could not attract men, but she preferred to avoid them. In her younger days, Dr. Biswas was attracted to her and was likely to propose marriage to her, but she was too preoccupied with her family to think about marriage. Dr. Biswas had encouraged her to have some time for her own self and not to slave herself for the family. He gives his own instance and argues: "I can't be a slave to my mother. We must be ourselves. You must go out, have a little rest, some refreshment." (87) From the very beginning she had a missionary zeal in her character and her ideals were Florence Nightingale and Joan of Arc. In the missionary school where Tara and Bim had studied, the latter had shown enthusiasm in going to the hospital to distribute blankets and fruits to poor patients and women who had recently given birth to children in the Maternity Wards. Tara would avoid such visits, and on the Thursdays (called Charity Day), she would make excuses not to go to school. Dr. Biswas observes that Bim seems possessed by a spirit of martyrdom which almost verges on masochism, representing the fervour that takes hold of the religious leaders or social reformer or family slaves. She herself does not realise her problem and it is Dr. Biswas who points it out to her. Once when he visits her house to attend Mira *Masi*, he says: "Now I understand why you do not wish to marry. You have dedicated your life to others—to your sick brother and aged aunt and your little brother who will be dependent on you all his life. You have sacrificed your own life for them." (97) But she refuses to accept this fact and in her confined rage "shook the thought of Biswas out of her," and later "she never acknowledged, even to herself that this ridiculous scene had ever taken place." (97)

Bim is one of the few seemingly practical women in the novels of Anita Desai who are strong-willed enough to face the challenges of life and to assume family responsibilities like a man. The narrative presents Mishra girls as her variation, who are her neighbours. Even though they are much inferior to her in respect of education and refinement, they too are the bread-earners for their families. The Mishras are a queer lot where women work and men merely waste time drinking whisky and going to *Muzaras* (song and dance of prostitutes). Ironically, the Mishra sisters married early, have had broken marriage; they were unable to adjust themselves to their 'advanced' husbands who are defence personnel and that brought them back to their parents' house for good. On the other hand, the wives of their brothers have deserted them and live elsewhere in New Delhi. Desai's description of the sisters is brutally acerbic: "Then the sisters cracked like old dry pods from which the black seeds of protest and indignation split, infertile." (38) Bim is a contrast to them who believes in her independence. Chapter III, going back in time, reinvokes the scene when the Mishra sisters' engagement is to take place. Tara and Bim apprehend the likely incompatibility that might follow the marriages. Bim feels, "I don't know why they're in such a hurry to get married? . . . they're not *educated* yet" (140), and tells Tara that marriage is not sufficient to last them the whole of their lives. Tara who is less mature wonders what can be anything more than marriage in a girl's life. Bim makes her intentions very clear, that for her marriage is not necessary. There are other things in life for her than just marriage:

> I can think of hundreds of things to do instead. I won't marry. . . . I won't. . . . I shall never leave Baba and Raja and Mira-*masi*, . . . I shall work—I shall do things. . . . I shall earn my own living—and look after Mira-*masi* and Baba and—and be independent. There'll

> be so many things to do—when we are grown up—when all this is over . . . then—then—but she couldn't finish for emotion, and her eyes shone in the dusk. (140-41)

Bim's father never bothered to educate her to be self-reliant, yet on her own she continues her study and finds a teaching job. She is a student of History and has a love for reading. She may live with limited means, but for books she could always manage money. Desai calls her a "triumph" and a "paradox." Her individuality remains uninvaded, her self-possession remains unruffled. And yet she could be prickly, introspective, self-appraising—painfully conscious of her limitations:

> How many students would laugh at me. I'm always trying to teach them, train them to be different from what we were at their age—to be a new kind of woman from you and me—and if they knew how badly handicapped I still am, how I myself haven't been able to manage on my own—they'd laugh, wouldn't they? They'd despise me. (155)

Desai's subtle observation brings to the fore the ironic misrepresentation of Bim and makes us infer the grossly incorrect judgements that the neighbours and acquaintances give in comparing and contrasting the two sisters as binary opposites. Tara knows better. She knows that Bim is as emotionally fragile as Tara herself is and also that Bim has suffered profoundly in the past. The characters of History like Aurangzeb, their agonized introspection and loneliness haunt Bim. Bim realizes that she has to take her own decisions in life and there can be no external help. When her father's insurance business has to be taken care of, Tara asks her to seek Bakul's advice, but Bim says she has to take her own decisions. The ending of the novel brings about a re-union of the family. In spite of the bruises, the betrayal that she had had:

> Bim could see as well as by the clear light of day that she felt only love and yearning for them all, and if there were hurts, these gashes and wounds in her side that bled, then it was only because her love was imperfect and did not encompass them thoroughly enough, and because it had flaws and inadequacies and *did not ex-*

> *tend to all equally.* She didn't feel enough for her dead parents, her understanding of them was incomplete and she would have to work and labour to acquire it. (165, my italics)

She is new in possession of decision, firmness and resolve. She would want to rely on her own resources; her revelations bring a knowledge that within every one there is light and shadowl good and evil, love and hate. Her expansion enables her to accept herself—there is nothing to be ashamed of, nothing to hide. Her life takes on the generosity and warmth that marks great love. She has taken a flight above her given circumstances and she could say, "I leave no trace of wings in the air,/ but I am glad I had my flight." (Tagore 1999: 382)

V

The seventh novel of Desai, *In Custody* (1984) probes the mental and emotional vicissitudes of a diffident, passive lecturer in Hindi, Deven Sharma, working on a temporary basis in a private college of a small town, Mirpore. The principal interest of the story is his fascination for Nur Shahjahanbadi, a reputed old Urdu poet and this brings about a series of comic and pathetic ordeals in his life. He has also written a monograph on the poetry of Nur, although it remains unpublished. His school friend, Murad, brings out an Urdu journal *Awaz* for which Deven has reviewed books. When one day Murad comes to Mirpore and offers Deven the assignment of interviewing the aging poet Nur, it seems as though he has been given a chance to enter "heaven," "the purity and immensity of his literary yearnings." (Desai 1985: 26) For him, Nur was a poet of "god-like magnitude."

Deven is a low-paid teacher who somehow manages to keep his body and soul together. He has learnt Urdu from his father who was also a school teacher and from him he also inherited the negative qualities of his personality, lack of self-confidence and timidity and he himself is placed in no better circumstances than his father and that is why he identifies himself with him in his dark moments:

> His father who had been a chronic sufferer of asthma and whose career had foundered upon his invalidism and appeared always to be apologising to his wife who had expected more from her husband and felt grievously disappointed at the little he had made of his life. As a child Deven had barely understood this but now that he himself occupied a not very dissimilar position at home, he felt protective towards the dead man, and in his imagination glorified and deified him as he had not done when he was living. At magical moments like this, the fantasy took on the stuff of truth. (73)

He has to go to Delhi to interview the poet which taxes his pocket, he cannot think of missing the opportunity though he is extremely nervous about his ability to properly interview the poet. The interview which should have been a matter of some hours drags on for months, leading Deven from one trouble to another. When his money runs out, he applies for a grant from the college and with the help of the Urdu teacher Siddique and the Registrar, he is sanctioned a grant to purchase a tape recorder, with the condition that it would be submitted later on to the college library. Nur's house is too crowded and noisy for the purpose and therefore a neighbouring house is rented for the interview. Deven has to bribe the elder wife of Nur for taking the interview. Meanwhile the younger wife of Nur puts one obstacle after the other, since she herself is a poet of sorts and because of jealousy does not want her husband to go on record in history through the interview. Murad cheats him by arranging a sale through a shopkeeper of an old tape recorder and also deputes a boy to handle it. But as luck would have it, when at long last the interview takes place the boy dozes off and misses out the relevant portions of the interview. Ironically, what could be taped was merely Nur's filthy abuses and irrelevant babblings about food, wrestlers and his glorious past. When he comes back to the college, some of his students agree to help him in editing the tape on the condition that he would show favour to them in marking their examination scripts. When he does not comply with them, he receives their threats. Meanwhile the college administration seeks his explanation. Pushed to such intractable position, he is made to appear deceitful. The lies, pretentiousness and contradictory circumstances drive Deven to pathetic failure and he ends up in the custody of ironic and malevolent forces beyond his control. Deven could very well be seen as a representative of ordinary man lacking adequate intellectual resources and insight to combat with the world which thrives on selfish interests and expediency.

Desai's method of story-telling in comic, ironic and occasionally stinging modes gets to the psychological roots of Deven's failures. She makes us see why he could never bloom into a balanced assertive personality capable of coping with the challenges of life. "All through his childhood and youth he had known only one way to deal with life and that was to lie low and remain invisible." (14) By nature he is 'tactless' and timid. That is why he is bullied and cowed down by everyone, be it his Head of the Department Mr. Trivedi or Murad or Mr. Jain who sells him a second-hand tape recorder or even his own students whom he cannot face with confidence, although he intends to be a sincere teacher. After a meeting with Murad in the beginning of the novel and in spite of being humiliated by him, he does not miss his classes. While teaching, instead of looking at the students, he "would look away quickly and focus his eyes upon the door at the far end of the room, the door that opened on to the passage, freedom and release . . . ignoring his class and speaking to himself or someone outside invisible." (12) No wonder he could not command the attention, "let alone win regard of his unruly class." (13) His tactlessness always lands him in unfavourable situations and he is not unaware of it. Lack of effective communication in the domestic sphere makes his wife suspicious of his proposed visit to Delhi. She thinks that he is going to Delhi to meet some girl. But instead of telling her the truth, he just keeps silent: "But that was how it was with him, he sighed: his reflexes, sluggish out of a habitual timidity and indecisiveness, were showing still further, tardy in both thought and deed. He was never ready with the apt word or appropriate action: both seemed to trail him at a moody distance." He is not only wanting in self-confidence, it seems he lacks the initiative, the drive and the pro-active spirit to rise in life. This is clearly stated by the novelist:

> Had he had more spirit, more nerve, more desire and ambition, then perhaps he would have instead hunted for success, distinction, magic. Perhaps he would have followed in pursuit of art, published a book of poetry, earned a name for himself, a little fame, even gold bangles for Sarla. (128)

Deven's love for Urdu and devotion to it, instead of being rewarding, antagonises his Head of the Department, Mr. Trivedi. The novel abounds in numerous debates on Hindi and Urdu. The two literatures deserve the right perspectives: aesthetic, literary and human. In Nur's house, during an engaging conversation when the merits of Urdu are being discussed, Nur's aggressive and hysteric passions surface. Urdu, he vehemently argues, is not only the language of lilting verses glorifying women and wine but much more:

> "I tell you, we must get over this rolling of Urdu verses into little sugar pills for babies to suck. We need the roar of lions or boom of cannon, so that we can march upon these Hindi-wallahs and make them run. Let them see the power of Urdu," he thundered. "They think it is chained and tamed in the dusty yards of those cemeteries that they call universities, but can't we show them that it can still let out a roar or a boom?" (53)

Nur's impassioned defence of Urdu and attack on its detractors takes an obscene tone: "Yes, alright, that will also be a kind of assault—on their noses anyway. Yes, let Urdu issue from any orifice as long as it drives them away." (53) The sane suggestions regarding the more practical use of the language is disregarded when a more practical man suggests: "Turn to journalism instead, Nur Sahib. Reach out to the people directly. We have a message for them. Tell them in plain speech. Use your power, for the purpose of attack and vengeance." (53)

When Deven goes to Mr. Trivedi asking for a week's leave to go to Delhi to interview Nur, he flares up and threatens to transfer him to the Urdu Department, not realising the sheer stupidity of his threat. The conflict of languages: Urdu versus Hindi takes on a political implication in Trivedi's outburst:

> "One week? it would be a relief to me if it were one year," bawled Trivedi, "and I didn't need to see your stupid mug again. I'll have you demoted Sharma—I'll see to it you don't get your confirmation. I'll get you transferred to your beloved Urdu department. I won't have Muslim toadies in my department, you'll ruin my boys with your Muslim ideas, your Urdu language. I'll complain to the Principal, I'll warn the R.S.S., you are a traitor—" (145)

None is willing to understand Deven's innocent love for Urdu literature. The muddled up value system tended to associate language with one's political allegiance and sectarian passion. Deven's love of literature is in a way a social handicap since he cannot earn as much money as a technically qualified man. He has to make the two ends meet somehow, facing humiliation from his own wife whom he cannot provide better things in life. Even students know it well that attending classes of Hindi literature has no practical return in life and they tell Deven that it is better to have technical qualification to make them technicians or mechanics and thereby earning livelihood rather than listening to lectures on Nirala's poetry or Prem Chand's fiction. They tell Deven, "Why should we waste our time learning Hindi when we can pick up some useful skills that will help us find employment? . . . Hindi does not help get you employment." (182)

VI

Desai's portrayal makes us see Deven's hero-worshipping and obsession with Nur as naïve and misplaced. Nur's poetry may be exalting and highly romantic, but as a person he is mean-spirited, hypocritical and stupid. He does not leave the opportunity of squeezing money, wine and food from Deven. Nur wants his "loutish entourage," actually parasites, being served with drinks and *Biryani* and *pulao.* Till the end of the novel, Nur's letters keep pouring in, asking Deven for money, for medicine, for his wife's treatment, reaching the point of absurdity, even demanding money for his pilgrimage to *Haz* and for the maintenance of his son, as though Deven is responsible for every ailment in his life, from his failing health to maintaining two wives and feeding his parasites. The absurdity of the whole expedition haunts Deven's mind like a nightmare. He has the hallucinations of Nur's funeral. He does not know what was the end of his life or if there was any end at all:

> Where was the end? Was there one? He had a vision of Nur's bier, white, heaped with flowers, rose and marigold, bright flashing flowers on the white sheet. He saw the women in the families weeping and wailing around it. He heard the funeral music play. He saw the shroud, the grave—open. When Nur was laid in it, would this connection break, this relation end? No, never—the bill should come to him, he would have to pay for the funeral, support the widows, raise his son. (203-4)

The slatternly description of Nur's household discloses profligacy, decadence and greed. The farcical undertone describes the crude games of power that the two wives play against each other. Filthy abuses float in the atmosphere. The elder wife is unlettered and her only concern is to browbeat the younger wife and in one episode the two fight alsol using most filthy abuses liberally. The younger one who had been a prostitute, claims to have literary talent that disgusts Deven because the verses that she recited were third rate and miles away from Nur's sublime poetry. Because of constant disturbance and interference, the elder wife suggests a separate house for privacy and peace for the interview. Without telling Deven that it is a rented place, she fixes a meeting with Nur stealthily. Deven has a hunch that this might be a rented place and his apprehension comes true when the rent bill is sent to him. The intersecting burlesque and intrigues serve as the parody of Nur's claim for greatness.

Desai caustically treats Nur and his likes like Siddique, an Urdu lecturer, in subtly driving home her cynical observations about the prospects of Urdu literature in India. Nur still lives in the past glory of Moghul culture when Urdu deriving from Persian flourished especially in the last part of Moghul rule in India. Even a late Moghul poet of 19th century, Mirza Ghalib wrote much of his poetry in Persian rather than Urdu. Desai traces the genesis of Urdu to the army camps. Certainly that grew with time but received literary recognition much later.

One may sense the novelist's contempt for the breed of decadent poets and their devotees who have not been able to resurrect themselves from the sordid conditions of the past and dead obsolete, decayed values. A devotee of this cult, Deven comes to a delayed realization that the hope for a wider world that he nurtured in his contact with Nur would turn out to be a kind of zoo abounding with predators and perverts.

VII

Baumgartner's Bombay (1988) lets us have a psychologically realistic portrayal of a displaced person, Mr. Hugo Baumgartner. Baumgartner has lived first in Germany and then in India, both pre-independence and post-independence. The novel covers a long span of time—from Hugo Baumgartner's childhood to his murder at the age of about fifty or so. It is the story of a man who is persecuted by society both in his own country and his adopted country, although for entirely different reasons. In his native Germany he is a victim of racial prejudice simply because he is a Jew. In India even though he has lived for several decades, he is still known as a firangi. When his father's flourishing furniture business is destroyed by fanatic Nazis, he is advised to try his luck in colonial India. He comes to Calcutta and for some time he does well in the timber business. In the meantime the Second World War breaks out, and in spite of the fact that he has nothing to do with the Nazi Germany holding a German passport, warrants his arrest as an alien citizen of a hostile country. He is put in captivity along with other Germans for six years in a camp in the foothills of Himalayas. When he is released after the War, he goes to Calcutta only to find the city scorching in communal frenzy coinciding with the partition of the country. He comes to Bombay and settles down there, living an ascetic life. In the late Sixties and early Seventies when India was littered with so many hippies or flower children, he is killed by a German drug addict hippie whom out of human sympathy he has taken to his house. Hugo is killed for a small amount of money that the hippie needed for his drug by stealing a few silver, actually a few silver-plated, trophies.

For having recovered a lost slice of history, the novel is hailed as a sensitive portrayal of a wounded survivor of history. Baumgartner's awareness of rejection and "otherness" began with his childhood in Germany. The brutality of racial discrimination dawns upon his childlike mind. Why his mother arrived later after all the mothers had left, with the coveted bourbon after school, why he alone was denied the Christmas present and why the word "Jude" printed in red across their shop window. The sense of inexplicable mystery and shame always disturbed him:

> The sense that he did not belong to the picture-book world of the fir tree, the gifts and the celebration? But no one had said that. Was it just that he sensed he did not belong to the radiant, the triumphant of the world? A strange sensation, surely, for a child. He could not understand it himself, or explain it. It baffled him, and frightened him even. (Desai 1989: 36-37)

In a dispensation when Jews were being identified as aliens, Baumgartner's parents were forced to put him in an exclusively Jewish school, he is ridiculed by children, being taunted "Baumgartner's dumb/ has a nose like a thumb." (38) He is misfit here because of his early secular and cosmopolitan upbringing. He fails to adjust himself in the school with

> The hysterical teacher who tore out his own hair and theirs [pupils] by the handful, the strange language in which he recognised only every third or fourth word, and the forbidding sound of the Torah. (49)

Baumgartner grew up during a period in European history when Jews were being alienated and persecuted with missionary zeal. The Nazi regime of Hitler was dedicated to the extermination and deracination of Jews. The details of different lives into which Hugo is propelled, the texture of the places, from the upholstered luxury of his childhood to the pavements of Calcutta and the scent of jasmine and urine are transcribed with sombre precision and unsparing irony.

The narrative gleans the pattern of sequences from Baumgartner's childhood when he belonged to a prosperous and cultured family. His mother, Frau Baumgartner, embodied delicate beauty and a cosmopolitan mind. Hugo remembers one of his visits with her to a relative in some suburb of Berlin where there would be talk of poetry, "an element in his mother's life that he understood as little as his father did," (48) and the talk about beauty, art and literature would be unending. Frau Friedmann "described a strange Indian poet whose work she had been reading, a sage with a long white beard and long hair and piercing, hypnotic eyes. 'A sage from Bengal,' she explained to Hugo's entranced mother . . . a book of poems was brought for them to see; . . . its title was meaningless to Hugo—*Gitanjali*.'" (47-48) Even a poem is dedicated to Tagore called "On Reading Tagore." But very soon the pre-Second World War German culture changes into parochial, fanatic Nazi regime. With the rise of the social Democrats, more popularly and notoriously known as the Nazis, persecution of Jews begins and his father's business is virtually confiscated by the state. In his quest to belong, Hugo ventures into other lands as an archetypal Wandering Jew. Hugo sails for India to try his luck. In Venice, where he stays for a week enroute to India, he wants to go to the Jewish Quarters, as though out of Germany he becomes more conscious of being a Jew and has the sense of Jewish fraternity:

> Strange, in Germany he had never wanted to search them [Jews] out, had been aware of others thinking of him as a Jew but not done so himself. In ejecting him, Germany had taught to regard himself as one. . . . Perhaps over here he would find for himself a new identity, one that suited him, one that he enjoyed. The air quivered with possibilities, ies, with suspense of quest and choice. (62-63)

Reaching Bombay, he is bewildered by Indians and their incomprehensible English. He meets Chaman Lal whose English phonetically is anything but English:

> Ex-pawt! . . . Ex-pawt. Of course, ex-pawt. Germany, Europe. Shipping, timber—I know, I know. . . . Chamanlal . . . began to

> talk of business, of exports, of shipping, of trade in what seemed to Baumgartner, a bewildering combination of two or three languages. (87-88)

On his way to Calcutta, two British soldiers are travelling in the same compartment but he "could not understand a word, was not certain even that it was English. They rolled their words in their mouths, like potatoes. They were as foreign as those children on the platform black, naked, raucous." (90) In Calcutta he is taken to be a Tommy, for to an Indian, any white man then seemed a Tommy. Late at night when he goes out to buy cigarettes, he comes across two prostitutes: "he was hailed by two women. . . . They wore white frocks, like nurses, . . . they smiled at him, waving 'Hoo-hoo, To-mmy . . . they grabbed him by an arm each crying, 'Less have drink, Tommy, come awn.'" (92) Baumgartner's complexion is a handicap for him because in colonial India he is taken to be a Britisher, a Sahib, a *firanghi* and therefore he cannot belong to Indians. He wished he could be darker but "Daily he grew redder. Would he one day be darker? It seemed desperately important to belong and make a place for himself." (93) But he would never belong even after his fifty years' stay in India. His tragedy is that after the war, his Germany is gone and he cannot go back there and his adopted country India does not want to accept him. When Lotte, a German woman who is his friend, and at times sleeps with him, bursts out saying that they are fools to stay in India "amongst the thieves, the cholera, the mosquitoes," Baumgartner rightly says: "Where could we go, Lotte? Where could you and I have gone?" Lotte agrees with him, "yes, there was nowhere to go. Germany was gone—phut. Europe was gone. All of it. Let us face it, *Liebchen*, there is no home for us. So where can we go? Hah? Tell me." (80-81)

But Baumgartner's greatest shock comes when he is arrested for being a German when the war breaks out. The Indian Police Inspector who arrests him is respectful to him and addresses him as Sahib and is apologetic, "I have to arrest you, Sir. War is declared and we must take you into detention camp. Very bad, Sir, very bad. . . . British make rules here, Sir, not Indians." (103) Baumgartner is relieved to be in the hands of an Indian, not a white man's. Even though Baumgartner being a Jew is persecuted by Nazi Germany, yet he is regarded as an enemy, an alien, because he is "German, born in Germany" and that is enough. He protests against this blind prejudice, "Yes, but of Jewish origin, therefore a refugee—" but before he could finish "He was caught by his sleeve and propelled out of the tent into a queue waiting to be handed into a truck." (105) From Calcutta he is taken to the Central internment camp in Ahmednagar where the 'hostile aliens' from all over India were kept. There the aliens were screened to find out reasons and ways to keep them in captivity. He wished to convince the authorities that he was a harmless Jew from Germany, "certain they would see he had been arrested for no reason, being harmless, no enemy, merely a refugee from Nazi Germany, who wished only to pursue his business interests in India." (106) But all this was in vain. He had more than one interview, spending many hours standing in slow moving queues, but it proved futile. All his arguments failed: "What am I to do then?" the man bawled when Baumgartner again protested at being labelled a German and 'hostile':

> Got a German passport, says you were born there—then what am I supposed to take you for, a "bloomin' Indian?" The papers were flung at him, and he retreated, baffled, wondering what magic world he might find that would release him from what was a monstrous mistake, or madness. (106)

The Nazi sympathisers in the camp bullied him and compelled him to raise his right hand and say 'Hail Hitler.' Therefore, he "was willing to go along with all these absurdities in the resigned, half-hearted way taught him by years of helpless submission to bullying, first in Germany, then in the camp, which was an extension of the former." (116) He realises that "silence was his natural condition." (117) Now that he wishes to forget and erase his German identity, his German identity pursues him like a ghost and makes him suffer in 'captivity for six years.' (107)

After the war is over, he is released from the camp and goes to Calcutta but now it is another city, a city reeling under communal riots. His old business associate Habibullah is perturbed at the new developments that would ultimately bring about the country's partition. Habibullah is also made the victim of riotous communalism besetting the partition. For him, India is finished, "Don't you know, Sahib, they are driving us out?" Baumgartner fails to understand because during his long confinement in the detention camp he had lost touch with domestic developments of the country and he asks who is driving them out:

> "These—these Congress-wallahs, *Sahib*, the Hindus . . . they say that will kick out the British. . . . And this man Jinnah, and his party—they are wanting partition, they are also wanting to leave. All Muslims should leave, they say. But—how? I have so much—my family, my home, my business—what will happen to it all, Sahib?" he cried, nearly in tears. (168)

He advised Baumgartner to leave Calcutta for Bombay. The communal riot flares up and the next day when he goes to inquire after Habibullah's welfare, he does not find him: "the office empty, ransacked." (179) Hugo is pained at the whole affair of communal violence:

> Baumgartner felt himself overtaken by yet another war of yet another people. Done with the global war, the colonial war, only to be plunged into a religious war. Endless war. Eternal war. Twenty thousand people, the newspaper informed him, were killed in three days of violence in Calcutta. Muslims killed Hindus, Hindus Muslims. Baumgartner could not fathom it—to him they were Indians seen in a mass and, individually, Sushil the Marxist, Habibullah the trader. (180)

He is concerned about Habibullah's welfare because he was good and kind to him and gave him business. When he talks about him to Chamanlal, he is given an unconvincing answer:

> Ah, my friend, you don't need to worry about Habibullah. Habibullah is much cleverer than Hindu *goondas*, Hindu thugs. He will have taken all his wealth with him—he must be in Dacca now, the home of his ancestors, happy and safe. (183)

Indian society, by and large, may not accept Hugo but there are individuals who treat him well. He receives warmth and respect and gentle hospitality from Chamanlal:

> Baumgartner could not discover why he [Chamanlal] took up a homeless foreigner, not even one with the prestige of having been an erstwhile ruler, a part of the colonial might and power, but simply a stray, a pariah in the eyes of the raj, clearly the most powerless of all. (183)

With Farrokh, a Parsi owner of restaurant where he goes for food every day also develops affection for Baumgartner. After Baumgartner's tragic murder, he cries bitterly. Though Baumgartner has resigned himself to the barbarity that arises out of ethnic and racial hostilities, the generosity of persons like Chamanlal and Farrokh provides him with the faith and hope that all human values have not perished.

Chamanlal often invited Hugo to his house for lunch. They would go together to the racecourse and bet on horses and win money also. On one such visit to the racecourse, Chamanlal collapsed and fainted. Baumgartner held his head in his lap till an ambulance came and took him to hospital. His son resented Baumgartner and threw such "furious looks at him as if he were responsible [for his father's illness] and then turned him out of the ward, insisting that he be left alone with his father." (205) Chamanlal died after an operation of tumour. It was a grim loss to Baumgartner. His visit to the cremation ground made him painfully aware of his tabooed presence:

> Baumgartner joined the mourners at the cremation, standing at the edge of the crowd, all of whom shrank away from him, horrified by the presence of a foreigner, a *firanghi*, at such an intensely private rite. Hearing the babbling chant of the priests, seeing the confusion around the pyre, smelling the odours of burnt flesh and charred wood under the noon-time sun, Baumgartner too wished he had not come, and shuffled away. (205-6)

Craving for acceptance and genuine human contact drives Hugo to find solace in the company of animals. He has picked up several wounded and stray cats from the streets and his flat in Hira Nivas is full of them. He goes daily to Farookh's restaurant to collect leftovers for cats. Every cat has a name and he talks with them tenderly: "He bent down and picked up the nearest cat—there was always one nearby. Holding its fur to his chest, he closed his eyes as a youngman might with a photograph of his

his eyes as a youngman might with a photograph of his beloved held close. Here was all the friendship he needed—or wanted 'Mmm, mmm' he nuzzled into the gray fur '*du Alte, du Gute, du.*' The cat growled a little, then began to purr." (151) People call him as eccentric and *Billiwala Pagal*. Desai describes his sentimental musings on the chart of his life in India:

> He had lived in this land for fifty years or if not fifty then so nearly as to make no difference—and it no longer seemed fantastic and exotic, it was more utterly familiar now than any other landscape on earth, yet the eyes of the people who passed by glanced at him, he was still strange and unfamiliar to them, and all said: *Firanghi*, foreigner. For the Indian sun had not been good to his skin, it had not tanned and roasted him to the colour of a native. . . . His hair would not turn black . . . what could he have done about his eyes? It was not that they were blue—far from it; his mother, holding him on her knee . . . had called them 'dark eyes, *dunkele Augen*,' but Indians did not seem to think them so. Their faces sneered '*firanghi*, foreigner,' however good-naturedly, however lacking in malice. . . . Accepting—but not accepted; that was the story of his life, the one thread that ran through it all. In Germany he had been dark—his darkness had marked him the Jew, *der Jude*. In India he was fair—and that marked him the *firanghi*. In both lands the unacceptable. Perhaps even where his cats were concerned, he was that—man, not feline, not theirs. He nodded thoughtfully; *Ja*, the cats, they always knew. (19-20)

Like *Bye-Bye Blackbird*, this novel astutely probes the psychology of racism. Nurturing prejudice against the people with different colour of skin or different shape of nose is a cultural phenomenon that prevails across continents, in advanced societies of Europe and in India.

IX

Lotte and Gisela, the two dancers at Prince's in Calcutta are the women whose survival and identity is linked to their sexuality in an alien land. Gisela, now Gala after the war, turns out to be luckier of the two, but to Lotte who chooses to live as a white memsahib of Sethia, the sense of belonging always eludes. Though she is not as sensitive as Baumgartner, she is seen as a promiscuous woman whom we meet first in the pre-War Calcutta, the British Calcutta with bars and Tommies. Hugo meets her in one of those bars. A Marwari Seth, Kantilal, takes fancy to her and she becomes his mistress and to make things less scandalous she is given money and a flat in Bombay. In his short visit to Bombay, Kanti would stay with Lotte. Kanti dies of ulcer. Lotte would request him not to drink, but he would not listen to her: "What did I come to Bombay for then? You, and a drink, that is my life, that is what I live for. Give me more whisky." (73) It is ironical that she has developed emotional attachment for Seth Kantilal even though she was perceived to be no more than a prostitute. Desai seems to be suggesting that the inner working of human heart does not always follow the dictates of one's practical mind. Lotte is a sexy woman even in the present time of the novel, a middle-aged woman with a "generous meaty triangle." (68) She would force herself on Baumgartner to make love to her, although he was not very keen about it.

Lotte is rejected by Kanti's family after his death. She is not the legitimate wife of Kanti, she loves him like a real wife. She has accepted some of the religious and cultural values of Hindus, like wearing gold bangles, symbolic of a married Hindu woman. She tells Baumgartner: "See, each bangle here is from Kanti: solid gold, twenty-two carats like Indian women wear. . . . Now I'm afraid these thieves will murder me for it . . . but I can't take them off and put them in the bank. It is like taking off your wedding-ring. Hindu women do it when they become widows." (73) When Kanti Sethia was alive, Lotte had a place in his family, even though rejected by Mrs. Sethia, the real one, the Marwari *Sethani*. Lotte reminisces about the old days when Kanti was alive and she would take care of his sons, like a mother: "Those boys—I know them when they were little. If they were sick, I made them porridge. At night I sat holding ice to their foreheads. . . . Not even a thermometer they had in the house till I went and got one. If they wanted to dress smart, I went and chose their clothes." (77) But Kanti's death changes everything. Lotte laments over the pitiable state of Kanti's death: "In Calcutta, I was not even there to hold his hand. His family was already fighting over the property—no one even to hold his hand, there in the hospital. Dogs die like that, in the street." (73) After Kanti's death, his sons refuse to recognise Lotte: "But when Kanti was dead, then they said, "Who is this woman? We don't know this woman. Throw her out." (77) Her case is similar to that of Baumgartner who in partnership with Chamanlal had bought a race horse, but after the latter's death when he approached his son to settle the issue of money involved in the purchase, Chamanlal's son coldly dismissed him since there was no paper regarding the purchase of the horse:

> "Show me one paper you have signed or my father has signed—" And when he says that there are no papers, the boy said stiffly, "My father is no more, Mr. Baumgartner. . . . He has left for his heavenly abode." (206)

Baumgartner understood that with Chamanlal's death "all connections with the firm, formal or friendly, had ceased, and got up to leave. The boy did not wish him goodbye." (206) From the world he inhabited, he sought the joys of friendship and care. Though he found himself hurled in several worlds, struggled with the knowledge that he has to live far outside the box of typical human existence, and yet he intended to learn to live, to love with deep fervour and wisdom. His life had not been unrewarding. It is not easy to identify with Baumgartner, however, one may draw from his story an understanding how the multiple configurations of history alienate not only an individual but also communities. His alienation and brutal rejection may have been brought about by his contingent location in history, but the betrayal, deceit and insults he suffers are the ones that any innocent, sensitive human being is likely to encounter in the human world. In rendering the tribulation of Hugo Baumgartner, Desai seems to posit her faith in human dignity not among the fortunate and the powerful but among the oppressed and the defeated. In spite of his existential thrownness in the flux of history, Hugo Baumgartner confronts life with strength and integrity.

Works Cited

Desai, Anita. 1980. *Clear Light of the Day*. Harmondsworth: Penguin.

______ 1984. *In Custody*. Harmondsworth: Penguin.

_______ 1989. *Baumgartner's Bombay*. Harmondsworth: Penguin.

Sethi, Sunil. 1-15 December 1980. "Anita Desai: Tremendous Changes." Interview. *India Today*.

Srivastava, Ramesh K. 1984. "Anita Desai at Work: An Interview." *Perspectives on Anita Desai*. Ghaziabad: Vimal.

Tagore, Rabindranath. 1999. *Rabindranath Tagore*, ed. Krishna Dutta and Andrew Robinson. London: Picador.

Uniyal, Ranu, 2000. *The Fiction of Margaret Drabble & Anita Desai*. New Delhi: Creative.

Chapter V

The Novels of the 1990s: Quest for Spiritual Fulfilment and 'Her' Stories (Histories) of Psychic Annihilation

The two novels written in the 1990s surprise us with the growing versatility of Desai. *Journey to Ithaca* testifies to Anita Desai's urge to connect her itinerant characters, Matteo and Laila with the spiritual realm of experiences; she creates visionary encounters beyond mortal awareness. As a widely travelled writer, Desai would endorse what Santayana says in his essay "The Philosophy of Travel": travel is wakefulness, like love it brings about a heightened state of awareness in which one grows mindful, receptive, undimmed by familiarity and ready to`be transformed. That is why the best trips like the best love affairs never really end." In *Fasting, Feasting*, one may sense the apparent semblance of Jane Austen's stories of a provincial family: mother, father, sisters, brother, aunts, preoccupied with love, matchmaking and marriage. This novel ironically unmasks the sordid, ugly truths of female drudgery and stifled lives of immured, circumscribed world of Uma, Anamika, Mira *Masi* or even Mama. The novel through indirections indicts conventional family values attached to femininity. What Sandra Gilbert and Susan Gubar perceive in *The Madwoman in the Attic* (1970: 103) is apparent in Desai's depiction of Maya, Nanda, Raka, Bim, Mira Masi. This novel even more forcefully portrays the process of anxious self-denial and social castration, the feeling of powerlessness and anger that afflict homely but 'homeless' women. In spite of being vastly different in thematic content, in both the novels, *Journey to Ithaca* and *Fasting, Feasting*, time and human personality dissolve in multiple perspectives.

II

The traveller characters Matteo, Sophie and Laila in *Journey to Ithaca* evolve through the journeys they venture into. Matteo's frantic search for flight recalls Arun Joshi's characters in *The Foreigner* and *The Last Labyrinth*—characters trying to live between two cultures. Like the protagonists of Arun Joshi's novels, Matteo has frantic desires for spiritual knowledge and the transformation it brings about. Som Bhaskar comes to a recognition that "Prayer does not change God, but changes him who prays." The kaleidoscopic cityscapes of the West as they travel towards the east make us behold the changes brought about in the consciousness of Matteo and Laila. The first section of the novel describes in ironic undertones the lives of Matteo and Sophie caught in the contradiction of values and desires. In a retrospective narration, Matteo and Sophie's journey recreates the west of the 1970s—the flight of young western people to India. Matteo, Italian, raised in the luxurious countryside around lake Camo, restless since childhood has been introduced by his tutor to Herman Hesse's *Journey to the East*, and it opens in him a desperate longing. Indeed Hesse's text is of the kind that has impacted a whole generation of youth, seeking enlightenment.

> Divine and eternal is the spirit
> Our way leads toward him whose
> Image and instrument we are.
> Our innermost yearning is to become
> Like him, to shine in his light.

Herman Hesse's *The Journey to the East* and *Siddhartha* and Somerset Maugham's *The Razor's Edge* were hailed by the western world as the epoch-making novels that sold million of copies and enamoured the entire age with magic and mystery of the east. Hesse's life and art were rife with multiple self-divisions, his writings of the 1920s are marked more than ever by the acute clash, to use Yeats's term, of fundamental antinomies—intellect and instinct, art and life, youth and age, male and female, despair and hope, time and timelessness, outsider and bourgeois—that he struggled to shape into coherent contrapuntal pattern. (Stelezig 1988: 18) Desai exposes Matteo to a state of dichotomy between the spiritual and the natural that continues to oscillate him in a state of indeterminacy. The narrative juxtaposes the past with the present, Matteo is introduced in the reminiscences of Sophie. The news of his illness brings her back to India.

> She was taken up the stairs to the upper floor and shown into the room where he lay on an iron cot, clothed only in pyjamas and the upper half of the body emaciated and moist with perspiration. Sophie thought he must be dying. (Desai 1996:1)

Matteo's sense of alienation has been traced back to his infancy "always in a hurry like a hare chased by unseen sounds. Not attached to either of his parents, "He stared at both of them and felt they repelled him equally. It seemed painful that they should be related." (19)

His story takes up the whole first volume of the novel blending the past and the present. Sophie's view of Matteo makes us see him, understand him and that renders her a position of an "eiron" who has watched Matteo's aspirations, cooperated with him and suffered his consummate dedication to the Mother.

> All you wanted was the mother; she reminded him passionately, You told me that. You said you needed the Mother not me, not the children. (3)

Matteo's early adolescence flashes across the narrative invoking the period when Fabian, an English tutor introduces him to Herman Hesse's *The Journey to the East*. The overpossessive, intrusive mother overhears the following that makes no sense to her.

> Is it that from some bright sphere
> We part with friends we meet with here,
> Or do we see the future pass
> Across the present's dusky glass?
>
> Or what is it that makes us seem
> To pick up fragments of a dream
> Part of which comes true, and part
> Beats and trembles in the heart? (21)

What is the source of exultation to Matteo and Fabian leaves the mother aghast. Following the guide book, Matteo, in the company of Fabian roams across the mountains, lakes, across architectures and histories of the past but what engages him most is Fabian's reading of Hesse's *The Journey to the East* and also *Siddhartha*. The company of books catalyze the dormant longing in Matteo for the vision, which was still unknown and distant. Therefore the prospects of going into banking at Turin or the silk business in Como are of no interest to him.

Initially in 1975, marriage with Sophie promises Matteo the hopes for enlightenment in togetherness. The description at the outset however anticipates the ironic outcome of this union, "Only Sophie still wore her hair very short and Matteo`was growing his long" (30). In their moments of departure to India, "in Matteo's pocket was the copy Fabian had left him of Hesse's *The Journey to the East*" (30). Like his predecessors, the "flower children," Matteo's attire is in conformity to his spiritual yearning: faded/ torn kurta, pyjama and chappal, like hordes of other Whites, he visits holy places. Clubbing with Sadhus, the holy men, visiting temples, worshipping icons do not as yet lead him anywhere. Visits to Ashramas and Yogis continue to confuse him until he meets the Mother. Her photograph inspires him with eternal bliss. When he watches her rapturously speaking about the Divine Light, he now discovers that "any time spent away from the Mother, without her, was wasted time, empty time, dead . . . in the mother's presence, he and everything else came alive." (104) And yet each moment of ecstatic joy would be alternated by the moment of self-doubt.

The growing differences between the couple, Sophie and Matteo, becomes irreparable. Sophie's role as an ironic observer debunks and undermines Matteo's endeavour for total devotion and faith. Nurtured in Christian faith, trained to take the Manichean view, Sophie's sceptic mind refuses to assign with the Mother the sainthood after knowing the Mother's past. Though Matteo tells her: "You should never ask questions about a Sadhu's past. They bury their past and are reborn when they take initiation." (125) Sophie impudently argues:

> "Ah, so—she was born, or reborn, the Mother of the ashram, and that's all there is to it, is it?" Sophie mocked. "But what if I told you what I've heard? What if I tell you she was once a dancer, that she came to India with a dance troupe. The dance tour went to pieces—I suppose the manager ran off with the money instead of booking halls or printing posters, isn't that what they always do? So, then there she was, on the lonesome, looking for a rich somebody to pick her up— (126)

In agitation, Matteo stammered,

> The Mother may have been a dancer, when she was young—I know that myself . . . but no one, no one has ever said the Master [the Mother's Guru] was one. I know because I am printing all the literature about him." (126)

Most of their conversation would end up on "Enough nonsense, Sophie." "Is that nonsense or a fact? Why isn't one allowed to discuss facts here?" (127) Matteo's quest for calm rootedness and spiritual elevation could not be fulfilled since setting a high goal called for paying a high price. His distractions and the rift with Sophie make him grudge his state of being misunderstood and impair his will. His renunciation remains fraught with uncertainties, because his desires are at loggerheads with his frail will. Mind alone is the cause of all bondage; the mind is also the instrument of man's liberation. One may draw from Matteo's story that faith gives us the possibility of seeing the invisible, believing in the incredible and receiving the impossible, but faith calls for the strength of will.

III

Laila's spiritual odyssey makes her traverse through a gamut of cultures: Islamic, Christian and Hindu across oceans and exotic landscapes. In portraying her, Desai identifies the restless yearning of those sensitive souls who live under the same sky as others but see different horizons, as the epigraph of the novel conveys:

> Always keep Ithaca fixed in your mind.
> To arrive there is your ultimate goal.

Journey to Ithaca breaks away from the traditional treatment of the themes of east-west encounter. Unlike them, it does not comply with a usually demeaning image of India with the idea of bolstering the white man's burden or a civilizing mission. Laila's encounter with India attains a mythical dimension—'a rite of passage,' in a sensitive tale of initiation, experience and the process of seeking enlightenment. Her readiness to know and experience the unfamiliar lend her a nimble mind, kill her prejudices. She comes across moments in her journey when she is on the verge of losing herself but she travels across and beyond such phases to find herself. Like the legends of Buddhist monks, who used to be vagabonds because they believed in wakefulness, Laila would come to a visionary's state in her consummate awakening. Laila's odyssey, "her experiments with appearance and reality," tend to communicate to us her narrator's curious findings into the realm of spirituality. Obviously, Laila's journey from Egypt, France, Venice to America and finally ending in India draws its specific details from her narrator's travels and sojourns and then "home coming."

Born in an agnostic and academic family in Alexandria, Laila's parents are teachers. But curiously, she is not interested in the dogmatic modes of pursuing knowledge, much to the worry of her parents. She is her own mistress and does what she likes which causes concern to her parents. She would roam about as a child and when asked where she was, she would say, "I don't know myself. I go down the street, I turn a corner—I don't know where I am." When her mother asked what did she do, strange was her answer, "'Do? I do nothing. . . . I walk, I play, I look. But I do nothing.'" (Desai 1996: 188) She is sent to Cairo for schooling. There she comes in contact with Muslim girls and although she is not much interested in institutionalized religion, yet she joins Koran classes. Instead of joining Westernized girls, she prefers to make friends with a single devout Muslim girl Fatima, and with her goes to the Mullah who teaches recitation of Koran. She wondered about Fatima, "What was this creature, a good Muslim? It had never ventured into her parent's agnostic, academic home." (163) The Koran class was different from the

French classes where pupils took the liberty of giggling and winking: "No one took such liberties with the Mullah. The girls kept their eyes to the written page . . . and Laila saw a way of learning that had no opening to debate, discussion, doubt or argument as it had been in her parent's home. Here was a book, a subject, a doctrine that did not allow questioning. It was powerful and authoritative in a strange and inexplicable way; it pleased her even as it puzzled." (163-64)

From Cairo, she is sent to Paris to live with her aunt for study. But here too, she finds herself out of place in the prim and proper household of the affluent. She hates the discipline of the house and behaves in her own defiant wayward manner to the chagrin of Aunt Francoise. She would live slovenly and in an "uncivilized" way and was called a "savage" by the aunt. She declares that she wouldn't eat meat and when insisted upon by the aunt, she bursts out: "I am a vegetarian. No one will make me eat the flesh of slaughtered animals. Do you know what you are eating? Have you been into a butcher's shop to see it when it is raw?" (178) In Paris she loses interest in French literature. "Even if Baudelaire, Rimbaud and Musset had invited them into this world once, the invitation had lost its warmth, leaving nothing, not even a scrap." (179) She preferred roaming in the Luxembourg Gardens and the Jardin des Plaubes where there were several animals in cages. There she cultivated a peculiar rapport with a panther: "Reaching out one of its gigantic paws, it dangled it before her, quite gently, as if inviting her to shake hands. . . . She began to smile, then laugh, as one might laugh at the play of a child, merging into its delight in a moment of unconsciousness, a moment when time either pauses or even moves back instead of forward. . . . They were the only two that existed in that enclosed world they had made. . . . They ambulated together, panther and girl, keeping pace, sending out messages of mutual admiration building a web between them of delicious complicity." (184-85) The relationship with the animals takes suprarational dimensions later when she would communicate with them in her Ashram in India.

In Paris, she is ill-at-ease in her aunt's house. Like good Christians, they go to Church on Sunday, but Laila prefers to move about in the cathedral premises instead of attending service. When the aunt asks her to accompany them to Church, she says, "I am a seeker after truth and have given up *all* orthodox religions. . . . I find them the repositories of ignorance and suppression." (199) It is this search that brings her to India though in a different way.

Her first exposure to India comes through the bookshop of Madame Lacan selling the books *L'Orient* and *L'Inde*. Here she browses through Hindu classics. At first she is attracted by the statues and paintings but later graduates to serious books on Indian culture and one day opens up the *Aitereya Brahman* of the *Rig Veda* and read what would become her own life, the life of a seeker:

> There is no happiness for him who does not travel, Rohita! Thus we have heard. Living in the society of man the best man becomes a sinner. . . . Therefore, wander!
>
> The feet of the wanderer are like the flowers, his soul is growing and reaping the fruit; and all his sins are destroyed by his fatigues in wandering. Therefore, wander!
>
> The fortune of him who is sitting, sits; it rises when he rises; it sleeps when he sleeps, it moves when he moves. Therefore, wander! (188)

Initially she is fascinated by an Indian dance troupe led by Krishna and she describes it to her aunt: "it was a dance of gods." (199) She decides to join the troupe much to the curiosity and a bit of scepticism of its leader Krishna. He doubts her suitability for the Indian dance, unlike the western opera or ballet, as it is not just the movement and music for entertainment. It is much more; it is spiritual, as Krishna says, "I have seen ballet—I have been to the opera alson It is entertainment only. Not spiritual, like the Indian dance. No spiritual side at all." (203) Madame Lacan is in favour of the European dance for Laila, "Laila can study dance here in Paris. Paris is the centre of the dance world. We have the ballet here, the opera also and the modern dance movement. Do you advise her to give up such fine possibilities and take up Indian dance instead?" (202) But Laila is very sure of herself and says to Krishna, "I will not be a European dancer. I want to be an Indian dancer." (200) But he has doubts. "So white, so small, Muslim. Egyptian. How can you be an Indian dancer?" (200) Even though she is accepted by Krishna, Vijaya, another member of the troupe, is bitter and sarcastic. "You think you are Indian dancer now. No Indian dancer must practise from childhood. Must have training. Must know our language, understand our music. Not everybody can be Indian dancer." (220) But nothing can deter her from her resolve to be an Indian dancer and she learns Indian dances quickly. From Paris, the troupe moves on to Venice.

In Venice, the troupe stays with the affluent Signora Durante who is a great admirer of Krishna and Indian culture. We are informed that Krishna is a Brahmin from Benaras, the holiest city in India. But Gianni, the housekeeper and chef is not impressed by the troupe. Irritated by their practice, he shouts, "Crazy! . . . crazy. This house has gone mad—dancing at night when the whole of Venice lies asleep!" (214) Ambrose, an Englishman and a friend of Signora calls on her. But his reaction is typical of colonial superciliousness. For him, it is not a great thing. He has no appreciation for Indian dance. "The Englishman did not seem to find the Indian dancer quite so wonderfully exotic as the Venetians did and the Indian dancer seemed no more enthusiastic about meeting the Englishman." (229) Whereas Signora's Italian friends like the Peacock dance performed by Laila, Ambrose has nothing but contempt and sneers, "Oh, not that tired old peacock dance again! They can scarcely pass that off as classical, can they? Why, it's what street performers put on in India." (231)

From Venice, the troupe goes to the USA and here comes the greatest disappointment. The sponsor Mrs. Du Best is not in New York and the troupe has a hard time. However, Jai Bhawabani of Bombay who owns Asia Bazar comes to their rescue. Their performance is arranged but the programme is thoroughly reduced and watered down to cater to the quotidian yankees. The American culture is childish in the eyes of Krishna. "This is America . . . we too must become children like them." (245)

Here clash of cultures is most telling. Herbert Moody, the agent who organizes their shows has no appreciation for Indian music and dance and he condescendingly declares it to be the general opinion, not his own alone: "That music you folks play . . . it just drives everyone right out of the theatre," he said flatly, "sounds like everyone of your instruments is out of tune. I'm just telling you what everyone says. No one's going to put up with that, or pay good money. Do something about it."

> "About the music of my country? You are asking me to create a music for American ears instead? To throw away my own heritage?"
>
> "Yeah, at least. While you're dancing for us," Mr. Moody said, without a bit of sympathy. (251)

But Krishna reconciles with the situation in order to survive. The troupe tastes another case of racial discrimination and white superiority at Holyoke where at a cheap boarding house, the proprietress says grace before dinner, "And may our visitors from the dark lands see the light and give up their pagan ways to follow thy path, O Lord." (256) By the end of the troupe's sojourn in America, Mrs. Du Best appears who "always meant to go (to India)—and have never been." Krishna says that she does not have the courage to go to India but Laila, now Lila, has. Lila is so committed and devoted to Indian culture that Krishna says, "India has always been her home. She has never been there, you are right, but it is where her soul was born. Her soul is waiting for her in India." (262)

From the India of her imagination, Laila comes to the real India. On the way she is "travelling eastwards to meet the great Sun, the great light. I must prepare my soul for the sweet union. . . . O mysterious India, I can feel you stirring in the dark." (274) But the real India is not what she had imagined. When she visits the Mahalakshmi Temple in Bombay, she is not impressed at all. She is not after institutionalized religion or rituals:

> This is not where I will worship—I cannot be made to worship what I do not believe. The truth is elsewhere. My search is not

> over. I must continue it. O where is my Lord whose calm face shines only with the pure light of truth? (215)

Her fascination for dance too is over. When Krishna tries to convince her that dance is worship, she retorts. "You have shown me devotion to worldly success, to financial gain, to fame—not to the true light for which I came." (276) Lila is hospitalized in a Missionary Hospital where a nurse, Mary, gives her a crucifix to make her feel better, but she throws it away,

> Do not give me that, Mary. Never give me what is so ugly and so sad. Do you think I need to have an image of sin and suffering? Take it away. I want joy and beauty and love. . . . I am no sinner. My dwelling place is not in sin and suffering but in truth and beauty. (281)

From Bombay she goes on a pilgrimage with Vijaya's family. She thinks about India and what she wanted from her: "what I wanted of India was the outward manifestation of what already existed inside me, what had been growing inside me like a flower grown from a seed I had discovered in a Paris bookshop of my past." (285) Seeing an ascetic sitting serenely under the holy banyan tree, the tree of eternity, she feels the great desire that she had always had "ever since I was a child, to be free of this world and escape into another, a better and brighter." (286) She reaches moments of revelation, a very personal mystic experience of union with the Lord, reminding us of Tagore's *Gitanjali*. In her Guru, she finds her Ithaca and in him she realizes 'Him': "Here I dwell now where I was always meant to dwell and where I resolve to live, never leaving His side. His true Devotee and lover." (293)

Laila's spiritual journey has nothing to do with religious rituals or orthodox religion. She begins to discover that a personal realization of oneself can only come from one's inner consciousness. As a Mother, she tries to clear the vision of Matteo. His faith can bear fruit only when he perceives the things from his mind's eyes. The many-sidedness of Indian religious tradition being Dharmic is truly beyond the theist and atheist categories. Its plurality and polycentric nature congenially embrace the whole world and all its beings where trees, rivers, animals and the stones inhere the cosmic spirit. In this Indian worldview, everything—*Characharа*—is a cosmic entity. Unlike the West, with no sovereign sense of evil, the most feared are also respected and worshipped, as the snake on the festival of "Nag Panchami." Man's kinship with the world of nature proceeds from the Karmic theory of rebirth; one may be born as an animal, insect, plant or a stone according to one's past karma.

In describing Lila's growth from Laila, Desai seems to be restoring or trying to understand her own Indian self. The awesome expansion of Laila/Lila's spiritual consciousness discloses the narrator's submission to the prospects of genuine contact with the spiritual India not just for a cosmopolitan insider but an outsider also. Her protagonist Laila's questing spirit experiments with multiple cultures, practices and beliefs in an untheorized space and finds that while the truth was ever new, ever changing, elusive and unfixable, India, her Ithaca could be a living *Sanatana*, home of enlightenment, where she could after all find herself.

Laila transcends the earthly time and space and in the sense Aurobindo visualized, she discovers the stairs of ascent and transformation and in her profound quest reaches the state of tranquil harmony with the Supreme Light—Guru unto herself. She has attained the status of the Mother who embodies the knowledge that the soul progresses from individual to community, from community to universe and from universe to infinity. True religion is the fulfilment of our nature.

IV

In the principal matrix of Uma' story in *Fasting, Feasting*, Desai records the stories of several feminine lives and draws almost a history of women's existence in the middle class India. In the second part of the novel, the frame of reference extends to draw the portrait of two American women Mrs. Patton and Melanie. What is made out to be visible is the fact that feminine lives across cultures are determined by the symbolic order of male culture (Chodorow 1981: 482-514). Uma and Anamika, like their variations in *Cry, the Peacock, Clear Light of the Day* and *Voices in the City*, evoke a young girl's growth to womanhood in the process of anxious self-denial and social castration. Uma and Anamika's vulnerability make them a female underdog; heckled and pushed by the dominant, punitive patriarchal processes, their defiance fails miserably. Helen Cixous sees such a situation as the outcome of "the politics of self congratulatory parental, conjugal phallocentrism" (1990: 320). Desai describes in vivid details what was kept hushed up—the histories of female exploitation. The narrative incisively penetrates into the essential loneliness of female adolescence and the years of growth.

Fasting, Feasting clubs two social contexts together. Within the larger framework of the lives of MamaPapa and Uma, Arun's sojourn to the United States directs the story to the Patton family. And yet the novel does not reflect the pretensions of east-west encounter as much as it illumines the lives of women across the east and the west. One would read in wider canvas of the novel the visuals of "great" Indian middle class; its aspirations, pretensions, values. The narrative takes a satirical overtone in the description:

> A meat diet had been one of the reactionary changes brought about in his life, and his [Papa's] brother's by their education. Raised amongst traditional vegetarians, their eyes had been opened to the benefits of meat along with cricket and the English language: the three were linked inextricably in their minds. They had even succeeded in convincing the wives they married of this novel concept of progress, and passed it on to their children. Papa was always scornful of those of their relatives who came to visit and insisted on clinging to their cereal and vegetable-eating ways, shying away from the meat dishes Papa insisted on having cooked for dinner. (Desai 2000: 32-33)

Uma, the plain, unmarried daughter is trapped at home, smothered by her overbearing parents and their double standards. Her story gains momentum when MamaPapa decide not to send her to the school so that their only male child could get proper attention and care. Mama is a perfect other half of Papa, totally enamoured of him and therefore any prospect of her evolving a bonding with her daughter Uma is nipped in the bud. The following description lets us trace the reasons of Uma's oppression: the so-called collusion of the mother in perpetuating, rallying, supporting male oppression of woman:

> When visitors came and enquired after their health, one of them would reply in the first and sometimes third person singular, but the answer was made on behalf of both of them. If Papa gives his opinion of their local member of parliament or the chances of the government in the next election, Mama said nothing because he had spoken for her too. . . . Their opinions differed so rarely that if Mama refused to let Aruna wear a pearl necklace to the matinee at the Regal Cinema or Papa decided Uma could not take music lessons after school, there was no point in appealing to the other parent for a different verdict: none was expected or given. (13-14)

Mama is a stereotypical product of male chauvinism who subscribes to the rules made by men. The consummate bonding of MamaPapa definitely affects Uma's future adversely. Around her years of growth lurked a confused knowledge of the secret nature of female sexuality. The cohabiting parents in their hypocritical ways kept their sexual relationship a matter of "open secret," planting a sense of shame in the daughter's mind:

> No doors were ever shut in their household: closed doors meant secrets, nasty secrets, impermissible. It meant authority would come stalking in and make a search to seize upon the nastiness, the unclean blot. Unclean with human blood. Woman's blood. But when it came to parents, one did not look. One looked down at oneself, ashamed. (15-16)

The birth of a son, Arun, to Mama and Papa laid a huge burden on innocent, clumsy, undependable Uma. Her music lessons were stopped, so was her schooling. "We are not sending you back to school, Uma. You are staying at home to help with Arun." (18)

School life to Uma was associated with the prospects of wholesome relationship, of purity, harmony, order, that the slovenly routine of drudgery fraught with double standards at home did not allow:

> The visible details would have sounded banal: the strict rules of the morning assembly to which the girls were not admitted unless they had been examined at the door to see if their shoes were polished, their fingernails short and without paint, the ribbons on their hair white and not coloured; then the piano on which sister Teresa banged out the hymns . . . the wonderfully still and composed figure of Mother Agnes . . . holding the prayer book from which she read in her deep unhurried voice that seemed to move between the girls like a slow brown river; the orderliness of her office room to which Uma was fairly frequently sent with a note from the teacher and where she looked around avidly, at the picture on the wall of a golden-haired Jesus holding a lamb, the tinted print over the mantelpiece of the tear-stained face of a child gazing up at a corner of the gilt frame where a silver star stone, or the polished brass vase with its spray of stiff fresh flowers on the desk and the clean white linen runners on top of the bookshelf, the immense clock near the door immensely ticking, and the view from the window of a garden of marvellous tidiness, the long verandas enclosing a courtyard that they could look on but not jump into because the grass was so precious and the roses so rare. (19)

The images of her school so vividly lodged in her mind create an intense desolation of spirit—the thought that she would no longer be a part of the school is unbearable. Everything about the school was a cherished part of her existence though she was not a bright student and that gave Mama solid reason to deny schooling to her, "You know you failed your exams again. You're not being moved up. What's the use of going back to school? Stay at home and look after your baby brother." (21)

Abounding in irony, Desai's narration takes ample opportunity to`describe a subsequent event. Uma's frantic hope that a personal meeting and entreaty to the Mother would help her seek Mother's intervention in the matter of restoring her schooling fails miserably:

> 'Hmm, hmm,' she said listening to Uma's sobs. 'Yes your fatherher wro me—I know. He says that because you have failed once again—' (28)

Then in utter despair, when the communication failed, she yelled and howled, the mother grew more hardened and detached. When she gabbled about the baby, not knowing how to bathe the baby, about being afraid to pin on his nappy, the Mother grew impatient: "Girls have to learn these things too, you know." (28) Uma was thunderstruck and the ironies multiplied when the Mother took out from her drawer a picture of infant Jesus sitting on the lap of Virgin Mary. The episode grew bizarre when, in utter desperation, Uma's frenzied cries turned into a fit of hysterics and fainting, she was brought up back home by the school van. The scene signifies that in a situation when a woman's loneliness injures her natural/rational ability to`express her emotions, her illness gives her away (Gilbert and Gubar 1980: 67). What is also worthy of observation here is that the parents's perception of their children inevitably affects persons outside the family. The contempt and levity with which MamaPapa describe Uma has already set the process of her social inferiorization. Quite a few readers have expressed their wrath at Desai's "misrepresentation" of an Indian family, however, a candid, honest rear view of an average middle-class Indian family during the 1960s and 80s could drive home the truth telling project of the narrator in unmasking the pretensions of the middle class virtues and indicting its sexist and chauvinistic bias.

Life changes, time passes; Uma is reconciled to rearing little Arun:

> She [Mama] watched over him like a dragon, determined that fixed quantity of milk was poured down his gullet whether he wanted or not and later the prescribed boiled eggs and meat both. Then when Papa returned from the office he would demand to know how much his son has consumed and answer had to be given: it had to be precise and it had to be one that pleased. (30)

V

In Mira Masi's rituals, vegetarianism and deep spiritual faith, Uma sees alternative modes of coping with the travails of existence. In the given world where women have limited choices and sometimes no choice at all, Mira Masi, a child widow, at least chooses her responses or feelings. In her devotion she chooses the possibility of *Ananda.* At the temple, she seeks bliss in her deep faith in the divine: "O blow the conch/ Light the incense,/ As the lord. Holding fire in his hand,/ Dances to the sound of the drum,/ On the burning ground" (58). Uma knows however that this experience of bliss is not gained by asking for it. Mira Masi, in her moments of sublime imaginings, rises above the mundane desires—in her free abandonment. Uma however is not so blessed, her own life she realizes "to have been full of barks, howls, messages and now-silence." (61) Uma's gentleness and sensitivity however does not die down despite the fact that she is not allowed to live life on her terms. The narrative reveals her reaction to the dying pigeon shot by the air gun of Dinesh, Aruna's son. She beholds the pain of the bird in images of an artist. In a ritual dip with Mira Masi, her almost drowning could be sensed as the subconscious desire to merge with the elements of nature—to die.

Uma meets with another jolt of betrayal in her marriage which turns out to be a farce. Her parents, taking recourse to the matrimonial advertisement, get her married to Harish, much senior to her in age. The fraudulent nature of the marriage is very soon exposed. Harish was already married having four children. His marriage to Uma was motivated by financial expediency. Instead of an escape, she is further trapped in ignominy and her miseries do not end because her parents would not allow her to become self-reliant. The offer to supervise a nurse's hostel of Dr. Datta is dismissed with contempt: "She [Mama] said, 'As long as we are here to provide for her she will never need to go to work.' But she works all the time! Dr. Dutt exclaimed on a rather sharp note, 'At home.'" (109)

Anamika's situation is no better than Uma. She is born and brought up in Bombay and has won the scholarship to the Oxford University but her parents cash in on the letter to get her a husband. After her marriage, she receives regular thrashing by her mother-in-law and that causes her miscarriage:

> Anamika had been beaten, Anamika was beaten regularly by her mother-in-law while her husband stood by and approved—or, at least did not object. Anamika spent her entire time in kitchen, cooking for his [husband's] family which was large so that meals were eaten in shifts—first the men, then the children, finally the women. She herself ate the remains in the pots before scouring them (or did Uma and Aruna imagine this last detail?). If the pots were not properly scoured . . . her mother-in-law threw them on the ground and made her do them all over again. . . . Anamika had never once been out alone with her husband. Aruna wondered what she did with all the fine clothes and jewellery she had been given at her wedding. (70-71)

One of the most self-contained segments of the novel is the episode of Uma's outing. Desai's caustic sense of humour and pathos invests this scene with the entertainment value for the readers. Mama and Papa appear as grotesque caricatures—the vamp and villain in a Cinderella story. The narrative gives away an uncanny knowledge of the trapped, arrested longings of a plain girl next door—the longing for attention, for romantic escape. Could one's heart block the sprouting of desire? Uma, the handicapped young girl strikes immediate bonding with Ramu, Bakul uncle's son. Uma suffers at times with fits—not conspicuously visible, but Ramu has "a club foot and wears an orthopaedic boot to steady him so he clomps across the terrace towards them. The bag weighs him down at one arm so his progress is slow" (46). The young pair of cousins feel at home in each other's company. Some dramatic scenes describe how once in her lifetime Ramu's company provides Uma with magical moments despite her parents' resentment.

> 'I'll take you out to dinner,' he offers grandly, throwing out an arm in invitation.
>
> Papa and Mama's mouth fall open—their lips and tongues look white. Uma squeaks. To dinner? in utter disbelief.
>
> 'Yes, can't one get dinner anywhere in the city? There must be a restaurant—'
>
> 'There's Kwality's!' Uma cries suddenly, making her parents turn their faces from Ramu to her without altering their thunderstruck expressions: What could she be thinking of, suggesting din-

> ner in a restaurant? She has never been to one in her life; how can she think of starting now when her hair is already grey.
>
> Then Papa gathers himself together. It is up to him to prevent this situation from getting completely out of control.
>
> 'No need to waste money by eating at Kwality's,' he says sternly. 'No need. Waste! Kwality's—bah!' (49)
>
> 'Dinner has been prepared at home,' Mama adds, also coming to life.
>
> 'No, no, we must eat out. I insist. I will take Uma out to dinner. The best dinner we can get in this city. Isn't there an hotel, with a bar?'

These dramatic scenes of Mama and Papa, Ramu and Uma make us gather the repressive attitude of Uma's parents. With Ramu, however, she enjoys equilibrium and harmony:

> 'Oh Ramu-bhai,' she hiccups, 'You are so-o fun-ee.'
>
> 'I am so fun-ee,' he sings the line improvising to the tune of 'My Darling Clementine.' 'I am a bunn-ee.'
>
> 'Ra-mu!' Uma squeals, spluttering into her glass.
>
> 'Hop, hop, hop!' warbles Ramu, . . . making his fingers dance backwards, 'Funny bunny, funny bunny.'
>
> Uma is choking with laughter. She has laughed so much, she has tears in her eyes. (51)

Togetherness with Ramu suffuses Uma's life with giggles, songs and dances of joy. The moments are shortlived, but in those moments for the first time she gets a sense of her own self that dared to dream. Uma is punished for the freedom she allowed to herself: "'I had shandy to drink, Mama—and the band played—and Ramu and I danced—' / 'Quiet, you hussy! Not another word from you, you idiot. . . . You disgrace to the family—nothing but disgrace, ever!'" (52-53).

Anamika reminds us of Monisha in *Voices in the City*, both described in the images of chain and torpor suffocate all their life. Anamika ultimately commits suicide by self-immolation as presented by the family. It is suspected that Anamika is burnt, as reported by neighbours, by her mother-in-law in collusion with her son. In cold, casual, understatement, the narrative drives home the menace of the crime—which is a part of Indian cultural practice.

> What the husband said was that he had been away on a business trip and returned only that afternoon on hearing the news.
>
> What the mother-in-law said was that she always had Anamika sleep beside her, in her own room, as if she were a daughter, her own child. Only that night Anamika had insisted on sleeping in her own room. She must have planned it, plotted it all.
>
> What Anamika's family said was that it was fate, God had willed it and it was Anamika's destiny.
>
> What Uma said was nothing. (151)

What is more sinister is the resigned acceptance of such events of cruelty as destiny. Anamika's story is strongly reminiscent of Anjana Appachana's "Incantation" (1998) that interrogates the blind conventions imbedded in Indian cultural practices placing women in destructive power-relationship with the patriarchy. The tragic end in both the stories is attributed to "Karma"

VII

Arun has had a pampered childhood—his having grown as a vegetarian however causes his parents discontent. In order to fulfil the aspiration of his parents, he is sent to Massachusetts in the U.S. Arun has to vacate the dorm for the summer holidays and he needs to find a family to stay as a paying guest. His relationship to the Pattons, his host, reveals the contrast and parallels in the east and west. The narrative, further honed and chiselled, portrays the American society, the plenty and abundance: "carefully constructed gardens, the small beds of bright flowers, stone edged and stranded in huge stretches of immaculate lawn, the clipped hedges, the bird-feeders." (161)

The family of the Pattons however is the mirror of American life. Arun senses in each member a self-centred isolation. Their lives are mechanical. Mr. Patton must bring large chunks of beef to barb-e-que every evening for dinner whether needed or not; Mrs. Patton must go out shopping and stock her already overstuffed refrigerator and freezer with more and more; their son Rod must jog daily and sweat it out, while Melanie, their daughter remains deeply affected by bulimia, devours chocolates and then vomits. Psychiatry regards anorexia and bulimia as behavioural symptoms and traces the cause to extremely stressful childhood. Melanie's irritability and withdrawal are misunderstood by Pattons, though Arun finds it appalling; a cause of serious concern:

> In the morning he finds Melanie seated at the kitchen table, her chin lowered to her chest while her mother talks to her.
>
> 'Daddy thinks you ought to go outdoors and play games, Melanie,' Mrs. Patton says as she cooks eggs, 'You have such a bad colour. You're not sick, are you dear?' Melanie does not raise her chin or answer.
>
> Arun, finding it too late to retreat, tries to pour himself some milk and cereal as quietly and unobtrusively as he can. . . . Melanie's face across the table looks like a blotting paper that has soaked up as much water as it can hold: it is blotchy and discoloured; it saps. Does Mrs. Patton not see? (206)

Arun observes that his parents in India were not sharply different from the Pattons. Even they fail to understand their children. Each individual lives in his own world, there is no genuine exchange of feelings. Desai employs Arun as a reflector to cast her aspersion on the insensitivity of the two families: the Mamapapa's and the Pattons. Two attitudes, two behaviours; one of the west, the other of the east; one American, the other Indian; the Patton's total blindness to Melanie's deteriorating condition; the overpossessiveness and extreme dictatorship of Arun's parents. If family as an institution is a source of love and nurturance, it could also be an oppressive and hideous institution:

> Even in Mr. Patton, Arun saw a reflection of his own father: "he reacted by not reacting, as if he had simply not heard, or understood." . . . Mr. Patton somehow had the same expression, authoritarian and resentful, to forestall any opposition to his and stonily waited for it to peter out and disappear. "Once again, its grey vaporous chill crept into his life, like Asthma." (186)

Melanie has to be hospitalized. Arun could perceive in the situation an analogue of his own family situation, remembering the helpless struggle of Uma against a hardened authority of the family:

> Arun does see a resemblance to something he knows: a resemblance to the contorted face of an enraged sister who, failing to express her outrage against neglect, against misunderstanding, against inattention to her unique and singular being and its hungers, merely spits and froths`in ineffectual protest. How strange to encounter it here. Arun thinks, where so much is given, where there is both licence and plenty. (214)

Arun's diasporic experience makes him see his own self, his people back in India with greater awareness. It is the defamiliarized distance that hones his perception and bestows him with a sense of right and wrong. The materialistic culture of the U.S., he is afflicted with inexplicable vacancy. Fads may preoccupy them temporarily: shopping, sunbathing, vegetarianism or Yoga. He could escape the nastiness, the stupidity of home, but what is replaced is hardly what he genuinely craved for:

> No he had not escaped. He had travelled and he had stumbled into what was like a plastic representation of what he had known at home; not the real thing—which was plain, unbeautiful misshapen; fraught and compromised—but the unreal thing—clean, bright, gleaming without taste, savour or nourishment. (185)

At the core of social familial gatherings hedonistic go-getting in India or in the West, Desai discerns artificiality, emotional void and pathetic aloneness.

VII

The long historical insistence on the otherness of woman, her core of feminine mystery makes woman (a beautiful woman) the natural focus of an art. Literature may particularly be seen as histories of beautiful, desirable women, where ordinary or not so beautiful woman is seemingly an exception, without any friend, while beautiful woman is always the subject of male gaze and perennial attention. Desai's narrative fights for the rights of Uma in debunking or subverting the values of patriarchy, Uma's secret desire for self-fulfilment are by no means measured in terms of right or wrong, but as her basic birthright. Desai's woman seeks freedom not from femininity, but from the blind and dead conventions, the cunning expediency of domestic-familial institution that reduce her to a commodity. Uma may be overtly submissive but her real self is recalcitrant, frantically seeking freedom. In a situation when the society perpetually administers its gravitating influence and grip over the despairing self, enmeshed in the muddled up intricate social texture, Desai describes the struggle of the individual for self-worth and if it is not possible then for escape. 'It is the drama of the struggling, faltering self facing the terror of single-handed ferocious assaults of existence" (Dalmia 1979: 13) that grip Desai's imagination.

Like all other stories of Desai, *Fasting, Feasting* testifies to its narrator's immense sympathy and emotional identification with the lives very distant from her own. The narrative chimes in with the vernacular of an extrovert milieu to make us behold the profound solitude of resisting, compromising, suffering, decaying. In the most traumatized, crushed bodies and minds, we read volcanic desires. The mundane social realism infusing the narrative manages to communicate the muffled tragedy of feminine lives—in spite of her withering ageing body, Uma's mind's eyes could see, remember and inscribe the history of several lives suffered and lived in anonymity.

Works Cited

Apachana, Anjan. 1998. *Incantations*. New Delhi: Penguin.

Dalmia, Yashodhara. 1979. "An Interview with Anita Desai." *The Times of India*, April 29.

Cixous, Helene. 1990. "The Laugh of the Medusa," ed. Dennis Walder, trans. Keith Cohen and Paula Cohew, *Literature in the Modern World*. London: O.U.P.

Chodorow, Nancy. 1981. "On *the Reproduction of Mothering: A Methodological Debate*." *Sign* 6, Spring.

Desai, Anita. 2000. *Fasting, Feasting*. London: Vintage.

______ 1996. *Journey to Ithaca*. Delhi: Ravidayal.

Gilbert, Sandra and Susan Gubar. 1980. *Madwoman in the Attic: The Woman Writer and the Nineteenth Century Literary Imagination.* New Haven, Connecticut: Yale University Press.

Stelezig, Eugene L. 1988. *Herman Hesse's Fiction of the Self.* New Jersey: Princeton University Press.

Chapter VI

Descent into the Numinous Corridors of History: Travelogue/ Novel in the New Millennium

Anita Desai off and on traverses across familiar Indian milieu. Her recent novel, *The Zigzag Way* (2005) is set in Mexico, the city with over a million people, a large Latin American republic ruled by Spain from 1521 to 1822. Aztec and other ruins recall its Indian past. Most Mexicans are descended from the Indians and Spaniards. Much of the mountainous landscape stretches across the country. Two main Sierra Madre ranges enclose a fertile plateau where most Mexicans live. The pages of the novel weld a young American would-be writer Eric's journey with the history of silver mining, genealogy of characters, formation of Mexican culture through the centuries of migrations, revolutions, wars, Cornish migration into Mexico, personal histories, rituals, cultural practices, beliefs, realism and fantasy linking Mexico with Cornwall, New England and Vienna in kaleidoscopic images. Mexico has perennially fascinated anthropologists, writers, poets, travellers, filmmakers for its "Otherness." Scores of stories transcribe the social revolution afflicting Mexico. The emptiness, decadence and corruption of post-revolution Mexico where people sought gratification in sadism, violence, sex and death figure as dominant themes in Katherine Anne Porter's stories,-"Hacienda," "Maria Conception," "Flowering Judas" and also in the sub-plots of novel *Ship of Fools* (1960). D.H. Lawrence and Graham Greene's accounts of Mexico seem saturated with reference to several rebellions and civil wars, gory secrets of love, lust, mystery and pathos. Stunning picturesque beauty of Mexican landscape, its hacienda, silver mines, its highest peak, Volcano Citlatepetl, Huichols, Zarzuela Circus Company to "Mexican Wave" (the football ceremony) invest Mexico city with magic.

The Zigzag Way, a metaphor for the winding path followed by Indian miners to enter the pits from outside is a labyrinth—that Eric treads to discover his past. Eric's journey takes him to Doña Vera, a grande dame surrounded by acolytes and snappy pug dogs, inhabiting the imposingly gothic Hacienda de la Soledad, and this contact releases in his mind half-remembered stories, told in his childhood in Cornwall, England. Tales of mining available in the library of Doña Vera in exotic places of hardships make him have elegiac visions of the loss and deprivation of his ancestors in the midst of the turbulence of revolution. The archives and travelogues and also the uncanny revelations, "Shaman—vision—dream—trance—ecstasy" (Desai, 2005: 49), connect Eric with his dead grandmother, Betty Jennings. Images of zigzag ways, chequered lives, labyrinths, tunnels and dungeons abound in Eric's illusions and experiences. The keynote of the text resonates with the sense of dread:

> But now that he was following the trail of his own history, tunneling his way back into his ancestry, and the history of his ancestors, he felt for the first time the urgency—and the terror—of knowing. (97)

Desai's narrative reveals deep affinity with the European gothic. Eric's story / travelogue proceeds to unfold what Allen Gardner (1989: 13) emphasizes as the characteristics of the gothic:

> Indeterminacy becomes a feature of the settings, stressing darkness, incomprehensibly winding passages, subterranean rooms, or caves in castles or monasteries. Enigma is actualized in plots which foreground the puzzle, and dramatized in the curiosity of the hero/heroine or the withholding of information by those who are 'in the know.' Hope and dread are made explicit in the hope of love, and the fear of betrayal, or more brutally, lust and the representation of sexual abuse, torture and death.

II

Bespectacled, scholarly, misfit Eric, arrived from Harvard, is reminiscent of the 'outsiders' of Desai, particularly Matteo in *Journey to Ithaca.* Matteo is enthralled by the poetry of Herman Hesse in *The Journey to the East.* Eric's spirit seeks inspiration from the lines of Elizabeth Bishop that appear as the epigraph of the novel:

> Oh tourist,
> is this how this country is going to answer you
> and your immodest demands for a different world,
> and a better life, and complete comprehension
> of both at last, and immediately. (Arrival at Santos, 1952)

Emily, Eric's girlfriend's research project is to take her to Mexico. Her field was the forests of Yucatan where mosquitoes teemed and malaria was rife. The would be writer within Eric prods him to accompany her in this journey with the hope that Mexico will yield the impetus he is lacking, energize him with a new self-confidence and push him out of his comfort zones.

Eric's contrast with Emily is of special significance to the narrative. In an ambivalent relationship with Em, scenes and sights that are of no interest to Em, draw Eric. Desai describes this as the "disjointedness of their joint experiences":

> Eric found himself distracted by everything in the airport—the Kiosks displaying textiles bright with rainbow stripes and rainbow flowers, tequila bottles shaped like cacti sweets made out of cacti and fruit, and the arrivals hall which was swamped by more people with black hair and brown skin than he had ever encountered before, families embracing and weeping and laughing as if they lived their lives on the level of grand opera. Outside, he was faced with light that struck more whitely, electrically than he had ever seen on to a spectrum of colour unknown in Boston, Massachusetts—flat-roofed houses with pink and orange and violet walls, pea-green taxis and leaf green buses. When they reached the hotel where the tranquillising effect of splashing water in marble fountains was cancelled by the shrieking of birds of bright plumage in tall cages, he had to lie down, he felt the blood racing in his veins too fast. Em did not appear concerned. (24)

Probably it's the "otherness" of Eric's family that baffles Emily. Eric comes from the fishermen stock:

> Visit to Eric's family were always hasty, improvised scrambled affairs, infrequent and rarely satisfactory. Em, who came from a solid phalanx of doctors, dentists and surgeons in Philadelphia and its environs, so that her own choice of a medical profession seemed not only logical but inevitable, never could find such a link between the Eric she knew and his family which was, effectively, his mother's side of it. (15)

She perceives the visible strength of Eric's matrilineage: "It was his mother who had, in her direct and practical way, dealt with the problem of having a son who is misfit for a son, this pale, frail scholar within a class of hearty Maine fisherfolk. Eric's father . . . accepted the blame, as an Englishman and an intruder on the Irish Catholic tribe." (16) Eric, bored with routine research work is not an austere academic type, "how he could scarcely bear to look at the thesis he had written on immigration patterns in Boston in the 1960s." In spite of the generous grant, he is not inspired to work. Unlike Em who is so focussed, certain and sure, immersed in her work and would not approve of Eric's languishing:

> a disapproving frown on her brow as she observed him sprawling there, idle. It would creep across her face whenever she came from a long day at the lab and found him at home, in Boston, listening to Mozart or to Schumann, with the cat Shakespeare ensconced on his lap. (11)

III

Sierra Madre, whose silver mines were abandoned during the Mexican revolution in 1910-20 has been historically a site of interest to people across Europe. The excavation drew people from different ethnic groups searching for employment and wealth. Historians have accumulated extensive records of the ongoing plights of Huichol Indians, and the pre-Columbian Mexico; the difficult lives of British miners stranded far from their home in the early part of the 20th century. It is here that Eric is to discover his mores buried in mysteries. Its exotic ceremonies against the awesome ruins as well as the natural landscape, enchant him:

> Over this great field of volcanic rock from the ruins of the Aztec temples, the tricolour of Mexico whipped like a dragon in the wind from the mountains that ringed the city and were visible at the end of the avenue and street, benevolent and protective witches wrapped in dark skirts. Eric and Em were just in time to observe the ceremony of taking down the flag for the night by the platoon of toy-sized soldiers as stiff and smart as painted lead. (25)

Mayans and Aztec designs carved in gold ornaments, guarded by police, the pavement vendors, "proffering lottery tickets, safety pins, or songbirds, in stacked cages, the zapotec women from the country who spread out their bunches of dry herbs, their shrivelled scorpions and fried grasshoppers on little mats they rolled up and made to disappear as the city police roamed up in white jeeps" (27). Many more stunning colours, exotic shapes, sounds and gaudy, garish artifacts of Mexico strike him as so contrasted with Boston, "at the corner outside the cathedral fleshy dancers in costumes of brilliant feathers and anklets of jangling bells danced and whirled the Aztec dances for tourists with cameras, purses and pesos." (27)

Into the township of Sierra Madre, however, Eric finds that there was more to the Mexico of colour and romance, "its emptiness and petrifaction were indescribably Mexican too." (41) But as they drew close enough in search for Doña Vera, "to make out the first range of bullet-coloured mountains, a crater suddenly opened up in the earth as if a meteor had fallen and formed it; a white basin like depression appeared which had not been visible from a distance." (41). The annual celebration of the day of the dead was approaching. As he walks along the lake, the landscape assumes eerie forms suggestive of the stasis—of soullessness, joylessness:

> Egrets and herons stood stock-still in the shallows as if they were roots or branches anchored to the clay below. Everything seemed fossilized except for the ripple of light that ran through the scene as

it might in a mirage. On the other side of the lake, against the flank of the mountain, there was a long, low building of stone, on three sides surrounded by an adobe wall that blended in so perfectly with the land . . . alludes to the concealed secrets that this visitation might disclose. (42)

IV

The exotically beautiful Doña Vera's lecture on the local Indian tribe, though delivered in Spanish, abounds in names and places that sound oddly familiar. He begins to recall stories told by his Cornish grandfather who once worked as a miner in Mexico but when he tries to talk to Doña Vera, "She is no longer the fantastically attired and theatrical creature. She had appeared earlier at the lecture, she was merely a small wiry figure in non-descript Khaki who barely stood out in that overwhelming landscape." (43) Eric watched her as she talked to a young boy patting the horse's neck and flanks and steadying the animal "in jodhpurs and boots, her white hair tucked under a hat" (44). Eric notes that though she houses local Indians, she never speaks to them, "only of them." When she gathered that Eric was not interested in anthropology, in the Huichol Indian, rather a personal reason was brought him to her she becomes unenthusiastic. At the dinner table, he could watch her attired dramatically in Kimono, that conceals "layers of worn and lumpish grey flannel," unravels a chequered past having fled "not the Nazis, but her family's Nazi past, was difficult to forget notwithstanding how much she tried sloughing it off to emerge like some sly and secretive snake in its new skin." (65)

Crowds of US University researchers chanting the pre-Columbian past and peyote-fuelled visions appear like "missionaries harvesting souls." But what drives Eric is his private quest—tracing his family's history in the ghost town of Sierra. Desai's narrative proceeds to conjure the struggles of Eric's grandparents and their community. Now in place of the Cornish workers, the native Huichol Indians suffer the cruelty of the mines. When Eric inquires into their lives, he provokes the ire of their self-appointed saviour: Doña Vera—the Queen of the Sierra who is resentful of any reference to the past history. She "packages for the purpose of tourist interest the 'living culture': "That is my purpose, Sen—or to keep it alive. Post-Columbian Mexico" (57). Eric gets to know that she is the Austrian wife of a mining baron whose family usurped the lands of the miners and made them slaves. In spite of her formidable authority, he ventures to tell her about his private quest:

> You see my grandfather came out to Mexico to work for a mining company. He was Cornish, from a mining family, and, you see, the mines in Cornwall failed. I'm not sure of the date—it would have been the early part of the century—the tens or twenties—'he felt ashamed, he knew so little . . . but definitely in this area,' he insisted . . . because I recognized the names you mentioned in your lecture in Mexico city, the one I attended, I told you I attended. That's when I heard that you run this centre for studies of this area, so I thought I'd come here to see what I could find out. I heard your family too had a connection to the mines.' (55-56)

Even though she claimed that Eric was "misinformed," "whoever tells you this, lies' (56), she exploded in vehement protest: "I am not one of those who took their land and ruined it with mining and made them slaves" (56). "Artists come to my centre, and scholars, and seekers. Not historians, and not—she fixed him with a fierce eye—'not mineros!'" (58)

Eric's finding of a counter discourse: Carl Sartorius' history in *Mexico & the Mexicans*, however debunks Doña Vera's half-truths:

> that after the fall of the Aztec empire, the conquest of the country proceeded with wonderful rapidity, chiefly because the invaders hoped to meet with great treasure in every mountain they beheld. The manner in which the Indians were forced to labour in the mines is well known and their numbers rapidly diminished. (1856: 40, 61, 1128)

The narrative of reminiscences reveals the archival history of unscrupulous ownership, holding and sharing of immense wealth and opulence drawn from the mining industry:

> Even now, with Roderigo long since dead and buried in the family vault where no one visited him, . . . Hacienda de la Soledad, the house at the foot of the mountain from which the silver had been extracted that made the family wealthy, wealthy enough to own this hacienda among so many others. The others however, being occupied by his mother, his aunts, his sisters and brothers-in-law, nieces and nephews, uncles and cousins, had been so many extensions of the prison house in the best locality in Mexico city to which he had brought her, while the Hacienda de la Soledad was from the very first her own: no one else wanted it. (66)

It was indeed "a graveyard of history" (67)—when she first saw the Hacienda de la Soledad, a ruin of blackened stones, fallen beams and cavernous halls . . . with wind roaring like an unimpeded flood through its emptiness" (68). This place invoked terror and fascination, she has delusions of "the panting breath of someone quite distraught," and would be suddenly interrupted by the shouts of the Chauffeur: "Come back, instantly, I beg you. . . . There are rattle snakes . . . scorpions as big as your hand, shafts you could fall through" (69).

In Doña Vera's library, reading the *Political Essay*, makes Eric behold the zigzag paths of the miners:

> The Indian tenateros, the beasts of burden in the mines of Mexico, remain loaded with a weight of 275 to 300 pounds for a span of six hours. In the galleries of Valencia, they are exposed to temperatures of 22° to 25° (71–75° F) and during this time they ascend and descend several thousands of steps in pits of an inclination of 45° . The tenateros carry the minerals in bags made of the threads of pite. To protect their shoulders (for the mineros are generally naked to the middle) they place a woollen covering under this bag. We meet in the mine some 50 or 60 of these porters, among whom are men above sixty and boys of ten or twelve years of age. In ascending the stairs they throw their bodies forwards and rest on a staff. They walk in a zigzag direction because they have found from long experience that their respiration is less impeded when they traverse obliquely the current of air which enters the pits from without. (78-79)

Eric wonders: "Was this the world his grandfather had found when he crossed the ocean and sought out new territory." (79)

The leaves of the book make him know a lot more than Doña Vera ever wanted. He gets to know:

> Frequently they have to ascend a thousand or fifteen hundred feet, not by ladders but by means of the trunks of trees in which steps have been bewn. As tallow candles only are allowed in mines, the workman must shelter his light with one hand, so that the draught may not extinguish it, and have therefore only a slight bold on the other. He thus moves upward with his burthen, the trunk being slightly inclined, and secured by props every fifteen feet, the abyss on either side, into which a false step precipitates him. Indians have been known to carry up from five hundred weight in this manner, in leather sacks. (85)

Eric's obsessive engagement with his ancestor's past keeps intersecting with the accounts of tragic irony in the life of Doña Vera, her memories of the first visit of a child Ramon to Hacienda, with bruises and thereafter her growing fascination with him: "It was the beginning of a legendary friendship, irregular and infrequent but revived over some ten years, again and again—till, abruptly it ended." (82) The ghost of the past haunts her. The memories flash forth certain truths that only she knows—the bizarre story of Ramōn's death:

> the black Coyote that hunted her down at night. She nearly broke out again into the howl she had uttered on hearing of his death—senseless, pointless, falling from a roof he was repairing in his village (so his family said, while others maintained it was in pursuit of a girl who lived nearby, and still others that it was when he was being chased by someone with a knife after a drunken brawl and that he had taken too much peyote and run out of control, but what did it matter what they said?)—throwing open her arms to catch him when he fell. She had promised to take care of him—why had she not? (82)

The narrative of magic realism, rendering Doña Vera's imaginings recalls Ben Okri's novel, *The Famished Road*:

> The armoire cracked open, waking her, and in the dark, Ramōn the god appeared, no longer flesh, and blood but paint and mask and feathers, a wooden idol whose eyelids moved. They lifted, and the eyes that looked out were real and alive. They stared at her, lying

> on her bed, old and ugly and shrunken—because she too was real and alive. . . . Her wooden lips parted to smile—but instead of smiling they uttered a caw. The lips were beaks, painted beaks that cawed. It was not Ramōn but *Zopilote* pretending to be Ramōn, and it was leading an army of *Zopilotes* that was emerging from the armoire, two by two, in perfect formation. They were not flying but walking, marching, kicking out their big clawed feet and stiff booted legs that might have looked wooden if they had not also looked military. (83-84)

The harrowing remnants of Doña Vera's past come sprawling in the surrealistic narrative invoking the nightmares that afflict her and we are told that "After such a night, morning could only come as a relief." (84) Desai seems well-versed in comprehending the feminine aspects of the gothic and in her conjuring, Doña Vera becomes a potent producer of the uncanny—both as a victim and the agent—a woman who figures as a maze. Philip Frenean's "Home of Night" could aptly describe her secret terrors: "Funeral shapes, and horrid nettles grew/ . . . conspiring spirits whispered in the gloom,/ half heard, the silly secrets of the tomb./ With blood the trees were all adrip." (Gardner 1989: 91).

V

The library had until now not witnessed a visitor who could be interested in the book of mining. Eric finds more from Carl Sartorius' book: "Frequently they have to ascend a thousand or fifteen hundred feet, not by ladders but by means of the trunks of trees." (85) And now he gets to know the deliberately concealed and forbidden portion of Mexican past not the "packaged history of Huichol art." Driven by his search at the site of the St. Francis Church, he recognized:

> The stone tiles under his feet had been rubbed soft and uneven by centuries of shuffling footsteps, and when Eric paused, he saw the old man had finally arrived on his knees and was making genuflections in all four directions, one after the other, meticulously, while his daughter, if that was who she was, went up to the altar, to light a candle.
>
> A kind of indistinct murmur congealed into a single, massed hum and Eric guessed it was the prayers and confessions being

> mumbled by all assembled in the comfortingly dark shadows. (111)

Surrounded by the gothic spirals, dark shadows, Eric wonders:

> If all the confessions and all the penance for the world's sins were not being released here, in the murky darkness, and humming around him in an endless spiral. In the bright, bleak chapels of the north, guilt and sin were not permitted, but they seemed to have gathered here for refuge and to live on an unquiet numinous and murmurous life in the unforgiving dark. (111-12)

"Crepuscular and underground but also palpable" (112) the past invoked, comes alive here. He finds himself as if in a spell, following the woman to the tray from which she had picked a candle to light. He selects two for himself, walks up to the altar and lights them from the candles already lit and flaming there. "Then stuck the first, and after that the second, into a bed of warm, melting wax, saying aloud, as he did so, his grandparent's names: 'David Rowse' 'Betty Jennings'." (112) He finds himself taking a leap back into the history of his grandparents, Betty Jennings and David Rowse—their journey from Cornwall to Mexico. The tender love between Betty and Davey in Chapter 6 almost reads like a Mills and Boon romance.

> Betty did not saif what she saw awed or frightened or enchanted her but she did, in every line (her letters home) express her trust in Davey and her joy in being with him. (119)

Davey's day started at the mine. Like many of them he would "line up in pairs, had their names entered the mine, the voices of those who went in first spewing fainter as the ones who followed sounded louder, then fainter too, as if they were descending the past." (124) Into the deep dungeon leading them below they would worship an image of the saint—the saint of *trabajadors* decorated with fresh flowers, they would light candles for him, before going in different directions to start work. The pagan, atavistic rituals baffled Betty but Davey assured her that he would not take part in such rituals. Davey could not far long conceal the sinister nature of hardship the miners were subjected to. Labouring constantly in dark passages, secluded from the world, the exploitative conditions that subjugated them horrified Betty. She went on:

> 'Don't you think it is wrong? These poor people being made to make over what they earn back to the Company? By *order*?'
> 'It's not as simple as that, Betty.'
> 'Oh, but it is,' she insisted, 'it is.' (133)

Linking Freud's theories of the uncanny with Marx, Samuel Weber argues that relation to socially determined objective structures such as 'commodities' which, according to Marx, appear to us as 'sensuous-supersensuous entities'; or 'phantasmagorias,' representing 'both the objectified labor power of society and an ambivalent, antagonistic social relationship. (Gardner: 105) The relationship of the mining community with the owners that Doña Vera's heritage represented, reveals what Weber observes:

> This antagonism can be articulated in various ways: the commodity is both necessary to the reproduction of the producers (under a particular social system capitalism), and at the same time absorbs and consumes their physical energies, and thus embodies a permanent threat to their physical existence. And capital is also described by Marx in terms of the return of the "dead labor" of the past, which lives like a vampire sucking up living labour, and which thrives all the more, the more it devours. (*ibidem*)

The narrative invokes the time by cross-referring to the Centennial of the Revolution inaugurated by President Diaz. The carnivalesque spirit of Mexican cultural events: Orchestra of more than hundred musicians, playing of bands, "parades of floats from which beauties in Spanish dress tossed roses to the crowds, buntings and streamers blew from the lamp post and, in the evening, there were fireworks in the plaza for which the entire town turned out, Mexican and Cornish alike." But what took them by terror and shock was the news that spread with the dawn, the rebellion had broken out and there started widespread looting. When the attack came, no one was in the least prepared, many died. "They discerned that not all the rebels had escaped, the federals were living up some stragglers they had caught against the wall of the Casade la Moneda and were shooting them one by one." (133)

The Cornish community gathered at Mrs. Morans, since she alone had living space for them. Pregnant Betty clutched at Davey's hands, as her time had come "biting her lips and drenched with perspiration" (141) With Moran's help, Davey rolled her in blankets and carried her out to the last wagon to leave the village. Into this encampment, Betty's lifeless body finally delivered a baby. "They lost her, saving only the infant." (143) "It was the three of them together that dug the grave outside the walled precinct of the cemetery . . . by dusk it was ready and they buried her before the dark piling rocks upon the grave to guard it from Coyotes." (144) The minister took him by the elbow, reminding him he now had a child to take care of and escorted him to Hacienda de la Soledad. The Cornish party had left except for Mrs. Moran and the infant. And more fortunately for Betty's child, "la Bella Isadore had given birth a short while ago to a still-born baby, and on seeing the tiny infant wrapped and mewling in Mrs. Moran's shawl, she took it to her full breast." (144)

The time of Davey's departure occurred in the clamour of reports of riots and anarchy scaring away the engine driver. Pancho Villa and his band of rebellion were much romanticized heroes, the abandoned trains were their hideouts. Davey's train passes by one such scene where they have a passing view of the band of rebellions:

> They were ringed by a band of musicians fiddling away madly what some recognised as '*Adelita*,' known to be Pancho Villa's favourite song.
>
> As their own train passed slowly, cautiously by, they asked each other if that had been Pancho Villa himself—Pancho Villa who said to wage war by rail, moving his men, his stores, even a field hospital and a gallows for traitors, along the tracks laid by President Porfirio Diaz, now fled—and if this was a presentiment of the new Mexico, the one they would not stay to see. (147-48)

They were all scenes of an evil dream that he had to endure without knowing if he would wake from it and life would return to normality again. The eventual arrival at San Luis Potosi could make it possible for Davey to send a telegram to the Hamma family and thereafter for the last time Davey went to look at his son asleep in a cradle full of flannel and lace and found himself in a tangle of emotions" (149) before returning to the mines. At the mines, however, the working conditions worsened. Davey who had never touched a drop now drank heavily. The time to return home was now at hand as the war broke out in Europe. Davey, together with the others, left immediately to book a passage to England. His country was caught up "in a wild wave of patriotism." Davey joined the men who volunteered themselves for receiving training in the Army. He was sent with a division of Rawlinson's fourth Army to France. Dying would have been a release, but he was only wounded in the Battle of the Somme, and shipped back to England to recover. After having married Madge, a woman who nursed him, he brought his son Paul to live with him who was in the care of Betty's sisters.

VI

Davey's journey ends up to guide us to Paul (Eric's father's journey). After schooling, he found a position in Liverpool as a Shipping Clerk, lodged in a boarding house near the docks with several other clerks. The idea of flight—of escape—like his other mates fascinated him. In the 2nd World War of 1939, he went to volunteer, but was rejected on account of curvature of the spine. Once he gets a cheap passage to America, but it disembarked up the coast of Maine. In the fishing village of Maine he found a vacancy in a local fishing business and then on his frequent visits to the house of his employer, he meets Madeleine, the youngest sister of the family, and falls in love. Marriage with Madeleine gave a home to eternally homeless Paul and now he had no reason to escape. When Eric was born, Madeleine proved as protective of him as of the stranger she had married. On the visit back to Cornwall that she and Paul undertook when they left Eric with his grandfather "in the pebble dashed cottage by the sea, when he played with a toytrain filled with sparkling flakes of ore till his step-grandmother, entering the room with a tea pot under a cosy, said 'Now don't go filling his head with all that nonsense.'" (154) The "sparkling flakes of ore" however remained buried in the mind of Davie's grandson, Eric, that he had once found in Mexico's mountains.

VII

At Betty's graveside the meaning of his own journey is illumined to Eric. He wants to honour his dead like the polycentric traditional Hindu: "Coming out of the Cathedral he has to steady himself at the top of the stairs before he could descend them." (161) He walks towards the cemetery. As it grew darker, darkness was intensifying: "The long night, the increasing chill, the effort of staying awake and alert, all became overwhelming, more than he could resist." As he walked towards the whitewashed wall that marked the periphery of the cemetery, he could make out a path winding up between rocks and cacti. Here he has the fantastic vision of young Betty descending the stairs with ease. Fascination and awe coincide in Eric's sublime imaginings.

> She was preceded by a fragrance that was as fresh as the breeze that was blowing freely, not the heavy perfume of copal, tallow candles and funeral flowers but a much lighter, more natural one, of herbs like lavender, rosemary. (175)

Eric stammered, 'You—you're like a flower yourself.' She almost said shyly mistaking Eric for Paul. "You're just as I thought, you would be. Dark like Davey—like all men in Davey's family. Eric admitted, "I think they have come from Spain or somewhere. The narrative in the last pages follows the logic or fantasy. "Her eyes widened and Eric could see their grey transparent glaze." (176) She proceeds to reply to the question about his not finding the graves.

> Our graves? She asked, quite blandly, and pointed out to the hill she had descended. 'We're there. D'you know what they call it? Jew's Hill. . . . It was a place where they buried everyone not of their faith.' (177)

The woman beckons Eric to follow her to the place of the pilgrimage, the place where the peyote cactus is found and is considered sacred by Huichol Indians. When Eric looks up to call and asks her to wait, she disappears. Leaving behind chrysanthemums:

> They lay limp on the wall, devoid now of any fragrance. . . . There was only the melancholy tinkling of bells and a movement of the speckled stones that proved to be young goats which had come to graze.

Eric recognizes that the spell is broken, below is the living throbbing township, with the appearance of the Sun, the church bells begin ringing "calling the dead back to their graves" (179). Eric has after all paid homage to his ancestors.

Eric's surrender to the uncanny experiences/visions by all means "alien" to an urban Americąn sensibility enables us to make sense of a powerful comment on the nature of culture, "that people can participate fully and mutually in the same society, in the same universe of meaning, while having totally different (and untransmissible) experiences of the world." (Sahlins, 2000: 37)

VII

The keen subtle eye and tranquil elegant prose carrying the surrealistic stories of several lives lead the narrative through synecdoche into the dark corridors and cunning passages of the past unveiling before us multivalent colourful cultural histories. The conflation of accounts of mining, shamanistic practices, rebellion, wars, ethnic rituals, magic, ceremonies, history of ruins and devastation with the lurking images of the individual moments of loneliness of "wandering men and women" lend this novel the element of mystery that recall Henry James' travelogues-cum-novels. As an uncanny fiction *The Zigzag Way* weaving a conspiracy of perception and imagination, would like to haunt the readers: the individuals inhabiting this novel would remain numinous figures not fully realized as if in a kaleidoscope—who pass through the passage of time struggling, withering and dying. Eric nonetheless evolves as the quester of knowledge that the *Rubaiyat of Omar Khayyam* visualize:

> Ah, my Beloved, fill the cups that clears
> Today of past regrets and future fears
> —Tomorrow?
> Why, Tomorrow I may be
> Myself with Yesterday's Sev'n Thousand years.

Like millions of travellers, Desai's quester protagonists would cherish the dream of carrying within themselves the wonders of the vast expanse.

Works Cited

Desai, Anita. 2005. *The Zig Zag Way*. London: Vintage.

Gardner, Allen. 1989. *Uncanny American Fiction*. New York: St. Martin.

Sahlins, Marshall. 2000. *Culture in Practice*. New York: Zone Books.

Chapter VII

Labyrinths of Mind: Imaginings, Memory and Desire

Anita Desai's fiction makes indispensable contribution to the field of Indian literature in presenting highly variegated range of themes fashioned in strikingly new, unfamiliar narratives that demand unconventional mode of readers' response.

The liberal, humanist worldview imbedded in her narratives testifies to her exposure to not only art, aesthetics and liberalism but to psychoanalysis. The innermost dimensions of her characters therefore are made visible by the narrative of retrospection. In terms and references of depth psychology one may have deeper affinity and empathy with her characters. The portrayal of Maya, Nirode, Monisha, Mira Masi, Nanda, Raka, Deven, Matteo and Uma enables us to rediscover Karen Horney's (Brown 1974, 140-41) perception that "All genuine neuroses are based upon disturbances of character which have existed since childhood, and it therefore follows that mere removal of symptoms carried out by means of hypnosis or suggestion can have no permanent value whatever. Basic anxiety as a feeling of being small, insignificant, helpless, endangered, arise in childhood in the case of children whose parents fail to give them genuine warmth and affection (usually because of their own neurosis), and who therefore have lost or never experienced 'the blissful certainty of being wanted.' Unconditional love is an essential for the child's normal development, and when this is refused the environment comes to be dreaded because . . . it is felt to be unreliable, mendacious, unappreciative, unfair, unjust, begrudging and merciless. According to this concept the child not only fears punishment or desertion because of forbidden drives, but he feels the environment as a menace to his/her entire development and to his most legitimate wishes and strivings. He feels in danger of his individuality being obliterated, his freedom taken away, his happiness prevented. This fear is not fantasy, but is well founded in reality.

Desai's awareness of the cultural determinism that affects adult lives as portrayed in the characters of Nirode, Monisha, Sita and Uma lend these characters psychological reality. In order to understand Maya's necrophelia, the obsession with love and death, we do not have to grope into the dark, but equip ourselves with the knowledge that

> In an environment in which the basic anxiety develops, the child's free use of energies is thwarted, his self-esteem and self-reliance are undermined, fear is instilled by intimidation and isolation, his/her expansiveness is warped through brutality or overprotective love. (*ibid.*)

Maya, brought up in such an environment (See Chapter II), grows up feeling that the world is a frightening place. In her relation to Gautama, she undergoes most frequently the processes of inferiorization. One such glaring example occurs when Gautama declares that she possessed a "third rate poetess' mind" (113). The unease disturbing her is tangible in the opening pages, "I found myself rushing out and appearing breathlessly in their midst—the midst of this charmed circle of leisurely gentlemen so comfortably, secure male, laughing, talking, drinking, generally drinking themselves into delight" (103). Gautama saw no value in anything less than the ideas and theories born of human and, preferably male brains. (90) Gautama's acquaintances are alien to her. The narrative's reach into the elusive indescribable rhythm and tensions in relationship is awesome:

> And so we strolled up and down the lawn, talking desultorily, not really listening to each other, being intent, on our own path which, however ran parallel and closely enough for us to briefly brush against each other, now and then, reminding us—or perhaps only

> myself—of the peace that comes from companion life alone, from brother flesh. (Desai 1963: 18)

One is reminded of Virginia Woolf's *To the Lighthouse*, one of the most sensitively drawn portraits of marriage that succeeds in mediating all the diverse strands, man and woman relationship over time, subjectivity and relationship, life and art. Who could be a better example of a married woman than Mrs. Ramsay:

> Nothing seems to have merged. They all sat separate. And the whole of the effort of merging and flowing and creating rested on her. Again she felt, as a fact without hostility, the sterility of men, for if she did not do it nobody would do it . . . as so giving herself to the little shake that one gives a watch that has stopped, the old familiar pulse began beating, as the watch begins tickling—one, two, three, one, two, three. (Woolf 1972: 126)

The onus of sustaining a relationship is on the wife—Maya. Maya would want her life to be a *joyous* walk, willing to give and receive love. Other than the married life with Gautama, she does not have any other avenue to open herself fully to a meaningful life. The psychic distance between Maya and her husband remains unmitigated and her desolation resonates with self-doubt, repressed grief.

The death of Toto, childless Maya's surrogate child, infuses into the narrative the jagged, hysterical tones when Maya cannot bear the sight of the corpse, "She rushes to the tap to wash the vision from her eyes. She thought she saw the glint of a blue bottle and grew hysterical." (5) The grotesque images of death abound Maya's imagination:

> All day the body lay rotting in the sun. It could not be moved onto the verandah for, in that April heat, the reek of dead flesh was overpowering and would soon have penetrated the rooms. . . . Crows sat in a circle around the corpse, and crows will eat anything, entrails, eyes, anything. (5)

The pain of immured existence, is further aggravated at the sight of monkeys on the platform. The impact of any external stimuli stirs in her a flow of images. She is more sensitive to sounds, colours, smells. The peacock's agonized call for mating "Piya, Piya" echoes in Maya:

> 'Can you hear them, Gautama? Do you . . . ?'
> 'Hear what?' (175)

The inner grottoes and grooves oppress her with claustrophobic sensations; the narrative penetrates in kaleidoscopic images the innermost subjectivity:

> Long back bars at the window shut us in, and the thin walls of the small room locked us all close together. There was something furtive about our movements, a tenseness in our voices, as though we were performing a scene from a play in the confines of a cage, for the benefit of a heavily breathing though invisible audience. (67)

Maya has no other alternative but to hold herself back from experiencing, realizing her human potentials.

III

In *Voices in the City* it is through Amla that Desai makes us see the hidden nooks and corners of her sister's caged existence:

> This sister had wandered away into some unholy garden of her own, stood there now like one of these lifeless statues, on the brink of the stone fountain, and seemed not to realize that the fountain was dry and what confronted her was no ripple and tickle of cool water but only dry, hard flagstones. (149)

Nothing more could invoke the sub-human masochistic character of Nirode than the lines that he is "a dripping gargoyle, grotesque, offensive, comic" (54). The inner disquiet of Monisha is projected in her perception of Calcutta as a "*this* devil city" (117). To Amla, the 'harsh,' 'insidious' conspires against all who "wish to enjoy it, doesn't it?" (153)

The emotional vacancy that envelops the mind of Nirode also afflicts Dev in *Bye-Bye, Blackbird*, the reserve and silence of the city of London mocks him at his recluse status. In the smoggy, hazy twilight the isolation of the Waterloo Station invokes a sense of dull melancholy:

> As in the old film, the dialogue was blurred, almost inaudible, merely an accompaniment to the scene—words snatched away and sank into the haze of departure, the fog of preconceived absence. (257)

The city and the landscape in phantasmagoric images serve as the trope of the interiority of its inhabitants with cinematic effects, Desai's vision of city reminding one of Dominique Lapiere's *The City of Joy*.

III

The enigmatic mysteries of mind and its fragmented multiple selves figure in *Where Shall We Go This Summer*? Sita's vision is intruded by the image of a crowd of crows attacking an eagle, "wounded or else too young to fly" (38). She ascribes to herself the image of a "jelly fish, washed up by the waves, stranded there on the sandbar" (149). Ironically quite a few critics choose to read this novel as Desai's illumination of the prospects of positive life. In spite of nastiness, brutishness, madness, boredom, life should be lived. Pregnant Sita's vicissitudes find a verbal transcription hard to accomplish. During the winter of 1947, Sita, then a young girl, lived on Manori island where her father was a legend to reckon with. Her mother however once escaped into the dark depths of the ocean. Manori obsesses Sita in her middle years and she feels alienated from her husband and children. Desai's achievement lies in depicting the extraordinary craving of seemingly ordinary men and women. The loneliness and neglect Sita experiences is made delicately identifiable. Raman's arrival to Manori and stroking Karan's hair with gentleness stirs in Sita her own pent-up longing to be loved. Sita herself "ached to attract," she stared at him, "bored into him with her eyes, wanting and not being given what she wanted" (132). The glazed irony ingrained in the narrative gives us the glimpse of uneasy equations:

> He stared at her with distaste thinking her grotesque. Her face was so grey, such sharp grooves ran from her nostrils to the corners of her mouth. It was the face of a woman unloved. . . . But whereas her beauty had turned haggard through nerves, neglect and indif-

> ference. . . . He himself looked grey and lined and a backache still tormented him. How old they were, he thought, to be having another baby. (133-34)

The content of the novel, its circular pattern, are reminiscent of Doris Lessing's *Summer before the Dark* (1973). The journey of Sita in *Where Shall We Go This Summer*? and Kate Brown's journey in the paradigm of spiritual journeying are redolent with ambiguity. Alison Lurie (1973: 18-19) complains about the end of Lessing's novel,

> Kate herself, now restored in health and looks, cannot think of anything to do but return home—like the seal in her dream, whom she has finally restored to the sea. The only apparent result of all Kate has gone through is the resolve not to dye her hair any more. . . . It is a puzzling, unsatisfactory conclusion to what up to this point has been a brilliantly realistic, wise, and courageous novel. Both this fatalistic ending and the title seem to suggest that for most women there is no escape from the prison constructed for them by society and their own sexual vulnerability. Yet this ending is as incomplete as any of the earlier ones would have been, because Kate is an incomplete character. . . . A woman like Kate, provided with exceptional intelligence, courage, energy and charm . . . would surely have some interest, some ambition in life. Having achieved freedom, she would have something better to do with it than go into the dark.

With reference to the outcome of the itinerancy and sojourn of Lessing's Kate, when we consider Sita, we cannot help discern that both in their story-telling mode of probing their memories lend almost a mythic dimension to their journeys. M.H. Abrams however takes a view that "Lessing gives Kate the moments of spiritual awakening—in ascending circle, or spiral. The ending is suggestive of Kate's return on a higher plane of understanding and experience." (1973: 26) Sita's rite of passage in Desai's novel also culminates in images of circles and swirling:

> She looked out of the window to see him [Karan] running round and round in circles on the terrace, as if warming up his motor for the journey. Giddy from kneeling and bending so long, she felt herself whirling round and round as well, she felt the long, straight,

> monotonous tract of her life whip itself round her in swift circles, perhaps a spiral, whirling around and around till its very lines dissolved and turned to blur of silver, the blurred silver of the mirror-like window-panes. All was bright, all was blurred, all was in a whirl. Life had no periods, no stretches. It simply swirled around muddling and confusing, leading nowhere. (154-55)

A sombre recognition of this sort is indeed likely to bring about the desired detachment. Compared to Kate, however, Sita's condition is that of not being left with any viable alternative. She is in her present situation doubly trapped because of her pregnancy that renders her physically vulnerable. The period of gestation that she spent in Manori island in the context of her retrospection acquires double meaning. An awareness now descends upon her that the mundane boredom of routinized existence indeed drives one to escape but the escape into the past brings about encounters with unpleasant truths. The intense passions that possessed Sita in her quest, now evaporate. Not all lives are the charts of exciting happenings. The only thing true about most women's life is its dull continuity. The return to the island, therefore, remains a dream, the island within her soul remains uninhabited—lonely.

IV

Memory is 'Jubilee and Knell' as Desai quotes Emily Dickinson in the epigraph of *Clear Light of Day*. The memory narratives of Bim and Nanda make us participate in the subterranean drama of inner discordant forces of their lives beyond control. The graphic verbal correlatives describe the inner landscape of Raka and Nanda in *Fire on the Mountain*, corroded by the memory of unjust power-relationship with patriarchy that Kate Millett so sharply perceives (Abrams 2004: 88). Memory indeed is a knell to Nanda. Her desire for self-dissolution is rendered thus: "she would merge herself with the pine tree and be mistaken for one. To be a tree, no more and no less, was all." (4) Raka described as "shipwrecked," moves about in Kasauli like a 'soundless moth.' The image of predator abounding in the novel is not suggestive of the wild animals but of androcentric tendencies. *Clear Light of Day* makes us probe into the subject position of a woman struggling to speak out her experiences. Bim is deprived of romantic love which could have enlivened the cold arid zones of her virgin mind but also opened up new channels of life. Desai's narrative visualizes Bim wallowing in self-pity, torturing herself with the grouse of being sucked and exploited:

> They had come like mosquitoes—Tara and Bakul, and behind them the Misras, and somewhere in the distance Raja and Benazir—only to torment her and, mosquito-like, sip her blood. All of them fed on her blood—Now when they were full, they rose in swarms, humming away, turning their backs upon her. (153)

Bim's reminiscing of past is an attempt to understand and master the memories of corrosive emotional hurts. In spite of the limitations of her past, she attempts to create a new different future. She dispels the lurking darkness and creates the clear light of the day—a triumph of her imagination. Her seclusion hones her introspection, she makes her own choices in renewing, transfiguring, casting another pattern of her life towards tranquillity and love. We recognize in this process Kierkegaardian observation that life can only be understood backward; but must he lived forward.

V

Extensive focus on the social fabric surrounding Deven's life in *In Custody* reveals a world where moral competence is irrelevant and that compounds and complicates the personal problems of the individual. Deven's prospect of growth or outgrowing his circumstances are bleak as no fresh breath of air or gleam of sunlight is allowed to enter: "The neem tree outside Deven's house has covered the entire courtyard with its branches like 'a dusty canopy.'" (13)

'Dust' is a metaphor Desai employs to drive home the atrophied and stagnant life at Mirpore:

> The citizen of Mirpore . . . could not be blamed for failing to understand those patriotic songs and slogans about the soil, the earth. To them it was so palpably dust. (19)

The astute and shrewd observation of the decadent rural towns and the sordid power politics controlling and subordinating the lives of innocuous people narrated in stinging, ironic overtones, makes this novel worthy of being compared to Shrilal Shukla's *Rag-Darbari*.

The wry, ironic ending suggests that in order to seek fulfilling meaningful existence, one need not be in a symbiotic or obsessive relationship with the other "greater" or "superior" individual. An individual's liberation is possible only in a meaningful contact with his own resources. The irony afflicting Deven portrays the plight of an "underdog" crushed by the opportunism and corruption ingrained in the social mores.

In *Clear Light of the Day*, it is the bespectacled Misra sisters or Sarla, Deven's wife, in *In Custody*, who had the usual aspiration of her social background to own the three fs×'Fan,' 'phone' and 'frigidaire!' The portrait of Sarla, whose expectations about married life are destroyed, is drawn with impeccable touches. The depiction of the heckled, pushed, buffeted and hopeless existence of Sarla recalls Fay Weldon's (1987) acerbic stories of female lives of drudgery:

> The thwarting of her [Sarla's] aspirations had cut two dark furrows from the corners of her nostrils to the corners of her mouth, as deep and permanent as surgical scars. The droop of her thin, straight hair on either side of her head repeated these twin lines of disappointment. They made her look forbidding and perhaps that was why her husband looked so perpetually forbidden, even if he understood their cause. (68)

Desai's immense empathy for the injured and the insulted for the cultural "Other" finds verbal transcription in the invocation of the life of Hugo Baumgartner in *Baumgartner's Bombay*. Sometimes one writes stories and sometimes a story visits a writer. Desai remembers:

> When I saw this Austrian Jew in Bombay—I actually saw the man pottering around the streets picking up scraps for his cats—that I began to imagine his past. And that gave me the key to open the German world. And I was able to use my mother's memories of pre-war Germany and our own perception of the war far away

> from India simply as a set of rumours and news that came to us. (Libert 1990: 54)

Viewed only as a fictional construct, Hugo Baumgartner should inspire only curiosity, yet he deeply moves readers. W.H. Auden's "Refugees' Blues" flows with feeling for an identical state of destitution:

> Once we had a country and we thought it fair
> Look in the atlas and you'll find it there:
> We cannot go there now my dear,
> We cannot go there now.

The terrifying loneliness of Baumgartner is described as "shivering on a hot summer night" as abjectly as a dog who senses he is about to be turned out into the street" (133). Images of captivity, internment flow in the narrative.

Journey to Ithaca and *The Zig-Zag Way* testify to the formidable reach of Desai's vision. Both deal with the itinerancy and probe the atavistic and occult regions of experiences. Journey of Laila and Matteo brings them in struggle with the old allegiances, old beliefs. The quest for discovering their true spiritual identity exposes them to a state of existential "thrownness." Matteo's faith is beset by vicissitudes and vacancy. Notwithstanding the risk involved in one's spiritual struggle, the novel visualizes the prospects of the leap of faith: Laila/Lila attains this feat; grows into a realized soul. The novel posits hope in the possibility of genuine contact with one's spiritual core. In terms of the itinerant Eric's travelogue, the zig-zag history of Mexico appears in kaleidoscopic performance in the semblance of a carnival.

VI

In Desai, love is a precarious journey as Monisha muses: "if only love existed that is not binding, that is free of rules, obligations, complicity and all stirrings of mind or conscience then—but there is no such love" (135-36). The crux of Desai's novels from *Cry the Peacock, Voices in the City, Clear Light of Day, Where We Shall Go This Summer?* and *Fasting, Feasting* is the state of lovelessness. While most male critics have ascribed neurosis to Maya, Som P. Sharma's (1984: 145) observation is much closer to Maya's truth:

> She is not seeking a fulfilment of the mundane love but of archetypal love . . . longing for the companionship like that of Radha and Krishna. It is a communion that she seeks—the true marriage in which body, mind and soul unite—the sort which the peacock seeks when it shrieks out its . . . intense mating calls.

Shanta Krishnaswamy (1982: 250) too holds similar views when she says: "Her needs . . . by a husband who is incapable of "husbanding her in his traditional masculine role." Uma's lovelorn existence of subjugation and discrimination, discontent drudgery in *Fasting, Feasting* receives alternately warm, compassionate and yet detached treatment, perhaps this mode of narrative makes the novel a documentary on female lives, disempowered, suffering perennial homelessness in India of the 1960s and 70s. A few lines of Emily Dickinson speak volumes about her condition that millions of women have shared:

> Big my secret but it's *bandaged*
> It will never get away
> Till the Day its weary Keeper
> Leads it through the Grave to Thee. (1960: 1737)

Desai's principal interest in the institution of family surfaces in her unsparing excavation of the appearance and reality of family life which is supposedly a necessary institution meant for socializing and humanizing mankind. Katherine Anne Porter puts it thus:

> even in harmonious families, there is this double life . . . the one we can observe in our neighbours' household, and underneath, another, secret and passionate and intense—which is the real life that stamps the faces. . . . Always in his mind, each member is escaping, running away, trying to break the net which circumstances and his own affections have woven about him. (1970: 64)

Most of her narratives reveal how parental authority accelerates schizophrenic problems, either ingraining unrealistic expectations, or desiccating an individual of all potentials. In an average family as Desai observes, the true feelings, true experiences are condemned and attacked because they do not conform to the role models formulated by the society—by the sexual-social arrangements. Maya, Mira Masi, Uma, Monisha, Raka and Nanda, described in imagining of net, cobweb, snare hedge, tunnel tomb, poignantly reveal the psychoanalytical view of R.D. Laing:

> although ego defence is necessary upto a point, a constant need to defend against a cauldron of unconscious elements place great strain upon ego's energies, with resulting exhaustion. The ego, besieged as it were, from within and without suffers from anxieties about coping, while containing frustrated impulses. The psyche having a limited amount of energy finds itself sapped by excessive inner conflict leading to repressions, anxieties, frustration, longing, denials and displacement in feminine behaviour. (Turner 1980: 46)

The fictional world of the western writers, Margaret Drabble, Margaret Atwood, Joyce Carole Oates or Fay Weldon inhabits doctors, teachers, professors, researchers—characters who are economically self-reliant. In proactive combat against patriarchal dominance, several of them seek self-empowerment and endeavour to rise above their circumstances. Desai's women belong principally to the domestic sphere who fail to register effective protest against the dominant traditions, their standards and values demanding autonomy or seeking positive self-discovery. Desai competes with Shashi Deshpande in drawing our attention to those lives that lay buried, unread, infrequently noticed and mostly misinterpreted. Both reveal concern with the split self, with the sense of isolation a would-be writer feels between her social female self and her inner artistic self. They share a common understanding of women writers as having been traditionally isolated from a primarily masculine culture precisely through the elements—gender female experience, artistry, imaginings.

Against a poetic landscape—the universe of Desai's characters discloses lives intensely lived, passionately felt, shot through the colours and nuances of desires as she seeks to make language perform the impossible task of simply being without referring. In making her honed sense of human psychology prevail everywhere, she imagines deeply from within the aboriginal core suffusing the inner world of her characters with the "heat and violence" (Woolf 1990: 18) of the poet's heart.

References

Abrams, M.H. 1973. *Natural Supernaturalism*. New York: Norton.

_____. 2004. *A Glossary of Literary Terms*. Bangalore: Eastern Press.

Brown, J.A.C. 1974. *Freud and the Post-Freudians*. London: Pelican.

Johnson, Thomas, ed. 1960. *The Complete Poems of Emily Dickinson*. Boston: Little Brown.

Krishnaswamy, Shanta. 1982. *The Women in Indian Fiction in English*. New Delhi: Ashish.

Lessing, Doris. 1973. *Summer Before the Dark*. London: Jonathan Cape.

Porter, Katherine Anne. 1953. *A Day Before*. London: Collins.

Sharma, Som P. 1984. "Anita Desai's *Cry, the Peacock*: A Vindication of the Technique," *Perspectives on Anita Desai*, ed. Ramesh K. Srivastava. Ghaziabad: Vimal.

Turner, Charles Hampden, ed. 1980. "Jean Paul Sartre to R.D. Laing." *Maps of the Mind*. New York: Mitchell Beazley.

Weldon, Fay. 1987. "The Weekend." *Secret Self: Short Story by Women*, ed. Hermoisee Lee. London: Everyman's Library.

Woolf, Virginia. 1990. "To the Cambridge Women." *Literature and the Modern World*, ed. Dennis Walder. Oxford University Press.

Index